To past and present members of the
Lewis University community:
Your journeys to Lewis have transformed lives.

> **"**
> [God] willed to commit me entirely to the development of
> the schools ... in an imperceptible way and over a long
> period of time so that one commitment led to another
> in a way that I did not foresee in the beginning.
> **"**

Saint John Baptist de La Salle
Founder of the De La Salle Christian Brothers

Contents

Acknowledgments

We wish to thank the many people who have helped make possible this second volume of *Journeys to Purpose:* our funding partner, the Network for Vocation in Undergraduate Education (NetVUE), for generously supporting the project; faculty and staff members of the Lewis University community, for writing and sharing their stories, and for persisting with the project despite new demands on time and capacities during the COVID-19 pandemic; the Office of Marketing and Communications and their designers Jim Cowan, Lewis' Executive Director of Creative Services, and Caitlin Winckler, Graphic Design Graduate Assistant, for the beautiful book design and *The Encounter* photo essay design; Leslie Ansteth Colonna, artist and Lewis Assistant Professor of Art and Design, for sharing her concept illustrations of *The Encounter*—one of which serves as the book's cover—and generous collaboration in crafting elements of the photo essay; Miles Harvey, author and Professor of English at DePaul University, for facilitating writing workshops, both on campus and online, to help our authors reflect on and make meaning of their journeys, and Dr. Simone Muench, Lewis Professor of English Studies, for recommending Miles; Allison Rios, our portrait photographer; Alec Smith (www.alecmsmith.com), sculptor of *The Encounter* monument, for generously providing images and notes of his sculpting process for the photo essay; and Carol Wassberg, for generous help with editing.

We especially wish to thank our students for the privilege of accompanying them on their journeys.

Sheila M. Kennedy, Ph.D.
Director of DISCOVER,
Professor Emerita of English Studies

Br. Philip Johnson, FSC
Coordinator of Special Projects,
Office of Mission and Identity

Kurt Schackmuth, Ph.D.
Vice President for Student Life
and Chief Mission Officer

Introduction: Creating a Vocation-Calling

by **Sheila M. Kennedy, Ph.D.**

Director of DISCOVER, Professor *Emerita* of English Studies

Motivations

College students nationwide are increasingly encouraged and more explicitly guided to pursue a vocation or calling—i.e., to live and work with deep meaning and deeply generous purpose (Clydesdale; *NetVUE*). Such an approach to living and working has long been considered both morally upright and spiritually fulfilling, allowing one to be fully *alive* for both self and others—an approach that "helps us live better and fuller lives…marked by expansive love, generosity, concern, and service to others" (Wadell and Pinches 6).

As it turns out, this vocation-calling approach to living and working is supportive and worthwhile in more practical ways as well, "providing a buffer against the challenges we all face at various stages of life" (Vedantam, "Happiness 2.0"). For example, people who cultivate a vocation-calling experience important mental and physical health benefits, including enhanced mood regulation, less impulsivity, a greater sense of self-esteem, happiness, and satisfaction, and increased physical health and longevity. People also reportedly experience stronger "interpersonal appeal" or "attractiveness" to others. And, despite the common thinking that one *either* pursues a lucrative career *or* a vocation-calling, people with a vocation-calling report greater income and net worth (Vedantam, "Cultivating Your Purpose"). Cultivating a vocation-calling, then, is a holistic undertaking, one that meets core human desires and needs for living a healthy, meaningful life—one that more fully *matters* to self and others.

Lewis University's approach to teaching and learning reflects these deliberate, vocation-oriented values and aims—both spiritual and practical—and this book is an explicit part of that work: a collection of engaging, instructive, and poignant life stories written by members of Lewis faculty and staff describing what it's like to discover and cultivate a life-long vocation-calling. The book also includes a photo essay showcasing the creative evolution of *The Encounter* monument honoring the inspiring vocation story of St. John Baptiste de La Salle. As with the first volume of *Journeys to Purpose*, this second volume will serve as a featured text in the university's first-year Cornerstone Seminar, offering students object lessons and inspiration for "living vocationally" (Wadell and Pinches).

Definitions

The terms "vocation" and "calling" have been variously defined and distinguished over centuries and from numerous perspectives (Wadell and Pinches; Cahalan 2016). A useful contemporary understanding notes that "a vocation is an approach to a particular life role that is oriented toward…a sense of purpose or meaningfulness and that holds other-oriented values and goals as primary sources of motivation" (Dik and Duffy 427-28). This definition echoes the most invoked description of vocation, one that dramatically captures the moral and spiritual dimensions of 'living vocationally:' "…the place where your deep gladness and the world's deep hunger meet" (Buechner 118-19); or what Parker Palmer calls the "birthright gift of self" in service to others (10, 30). A "calling" includes the dimension of being *summoned*, i.e., a "transcendent summons…originating beyond the self" to pursue a meaningful, purposeful, other-directed vocation. Finally, another description of vocation-calling—both simple and rich—is captured in the book's title: a journey to purpose.

Questions

Together, the various definitions and descriptions may prompt questions: Does everyone have a vocation or calling? Does everyone have just one? What are the sources of a vocation or calling? What motivates the journey? What will the journey be like? What obstacles or challenges might one experience? Are detours inevitable? How can one best navigate the challenges, the detours? And journey to *which* purpose? What's worthy? What qualifies? How can one know?

The life stories in this collection respond both explicitly and implicitly to these questions. Each story offers a sincere account of what it's like to pursue a journey to purpose, one that is aligned with something authentically true about the self, is experienced as deeply meaningful, and one that often offers opportunities for experiences that are deeply enjoyed—i.e., they're both challenging and achievable— otherwise known as "optimal" or "flow" experiences (Csikszentmihalyi 110). The stories also convey how a vocation-calling can create a transformative, even sacred, impact for those on the journey, the people around them witnessing their aligned sense of purpose, and the people whom their vocations or callings serve.

Those beginning the journey especially wonder about the question of knowing: How can one *know* how to be and what to do? Two responses can help here. The first offers common sources or "pathways" to a vocation-calling. The second offers a useful, lifelong process.

Pathways to Purpose

Researchers have identified three common "pathways to purpose" (Vedantam, "Happiness 2.0"). Knowing these pathways, connecting them with living examples, and reflecting on how one or more pathways might resonate in one's own life can be useful

> **"**
> If it's true—that the journey to purpose is 'a creative act' (and it is!)—then that means we have access to a reliable framework and approach for the journey: the creative process.
> **"**

for discerning a purpose (or purposes—plural. See, for example, Wapnick on "multipotentialites").

The first pathway is based on a hobby, passion, or talent—"proactive pathways"—that grow over time. At some point, the person realizes that their interest gives them a sense of purpose, and they pursue it more intentionally. While most stories in this collection reflect a combination of pathways, examples of stories that reflect proactive pathways to purpose, at least in part, include those by Leslie Ansteth Colonna, Joseph Kozminski, and Megan Zahos.

In contrast to a proactive pathway, the second common source of a vocation-calling is a "reactive pathway" in which "something happens"—a major life event, circumstances, conditions—and the person is called into it, called to respond. Examples of stories from this collection that reflect reactive pathways to purpose, at least in part, include those by Tennille Nicole Allen, Jennifer Buss, Erica R. Dávila, Antonieta S. Fitzpatrick, John Greenwood, Morris Jenkins, Pramod Mishra, Roman Ortega, Jr., Michael Parker, and Michael Zegadlo.

The third common source of a vocation-calling is the "social learning pathway" in which a person is inspired by another person living with aligned purpose. Examples of stories from this collection that reflect a social learning pathway to purpose, at least in part, include those by Bonnie Bondavalli, Bryan Durkin, Melissa M. Eichelberger, Jung Kim, Michele Riley Kramer, Brother Joseph Martin, Michael Progress, Iyad Rock, Brother Larry Schatz, and Laura Wilmarth Tyna.Together, the life stories reflect a spectrum of lived experiences—hardships, insights, and fulfillment—conveyed with authentic and engaging images, language, and life-affirming reflection.

A Creative Act

In addition to illustrating the pathways to purpose, the stories variously reflect features of what it's like to be *on* a journey to purpose. That is, even if the source or pathway is evident, the journey itself still needs navigating for knowing more, clarifying, and taking next steps—an endeavor that may appear mystifying to young and old alike: *What do I do? Where do I start?* Theologian Kathleen Cahalan offers important instruction when she emphasizes that the journey to purpose is "a creative act" (qtd. in Wadell and Pinches 12; see also Sheldon; Vedantam, "Who Do You Want to Be?"). If it's true—that the journey to purpose is 'a creative act' (and it is!)—then that means we have access to a reliable framework and approach for the journey: the creative process.

The Creative Process

The creative process has been extensively researched, revealing common features and reliable patterns, all of which can guide the creative act of pursuing a journey to purpose. These patterns include:

1. Preparation: "becoming immersed... in a set of problematic issues that are interesting and arouse curiosity...." Applied to the journey, interesting issues may arise as one immerses oneself in particular content areas—for example, in a major, minor, or course—or in the developing of a talent or skill, or from personal circumstances or experiences, community concerns, preoccupations, or from a growing understanding of self, desires, and values.

2. Incubation: a period "during which ideas churn below the threshold of consciousness...when unusual connections are to be made," connections unique to the person making them. While mysterious, "the non-conscious mind" can be a powerful tool for experiencing insights for clarifying a vocation-calling.

3. Insight: "sometimes called the 'Aha!' moment...when the pieces of the puzzle fall together," insights which may be experienced throughout the process, throughout the journey.

4. Evaluation: "a period of discerning when the person must decide whether the insight is valuable or worth pursuing." For the journey to purpose, this evaluation includes discerning the extent to which the insight matches "true self"—our growing understanding of our values, authentic inner voice, and felt sense.

5. Elaboration: taking steps, trying out, acting—based on the insights, evaluating, discerning—and adapting as needed given what's learned (Csikszentmihalyi 80).

6. Repetition: re-engaging the various elements of the creative process as the journey continues (qtd. passages above from Csikszentmihalyi 79-80; see also Palmer; Reyes; Sheldon; Vedantam).

As you read the stories collected here, note the features of the creative journeying being described. How do the authors *prepare*, or what is the nature of their respective *immersions*? In what ways do they experience *incubation*? What are some *insights* they enjoy, and how do they *evaluate* or discern the relative rightness or trueness of those insights? Once evaluated, how do they *elaborate* or act on the insights? What's *learned*, including from the detours or disappointments they may experience, and how do they adapt or navigate? And how are they *repeating* or *continuing* the process, the journey? Finally, while the creative process and a journey to purpose are often characterized as individual endeavors, note the essential role that *community* plays as they creatively discern their journeys (Reyes).

Implications

There are numerous, useful implications for understanding the journey to purpose as a creative act with an accompanying creative process. First, it's helpful simply to know that the creative process is **"a thing,"** an established, evidence-based process that can help navigate the unknown, to create what can be, and to live, especially through the lens of vocation and calling. In turn, knowing that an established, reliable process is available may offer calm and confidence—*faith*—in and for the journey.

In addition, because the creative process requires active engagement, it offers and creates **agency**. That is, there are things we can *do* that can make a difference in the ongoing outcomes. This agency is why students are urged to do "all the things:" to meet and create relationships with people from a variety of backgrounds; join clubs and organizations; participate in activities and attend performances; double major or minor; intentionally enroll in general education courses, electives, and travel study; volunteer; develop talents; learn new skills—essentially, engage broadly and deeply, all of which becomes "content" to immerse in for the discerning journey. Agency through engagement—and ongoing reflection—is key for discerning both 'true self' and what to do *from* 'true self': Who am I, who do I wish to *be*, in relation to all these new learnings? And what can I uniquely *do* with this clearer sense of 'true self' and new learnings to meaningfully contribute?

Another implication: Because the features or stages of the creative process are often enumerated—as they are here, numbered on the page—the process appears chronological, linear, unfolding neatly in a prescribed order. Importantly, though, the creative process—and, in turn, the journey to purpose—is **nonlinear**. That is, the process is gradual, incremental, iterative, dynamic, adjustable, recursive—indeed a *journey*—with wandering, detouring, overlapping activities, recurring, all dependent on the person, circumstances, and acts of engagement and responsiveness along the way (Csikszentmihalyi 80).

Given its nonlinear nature, instead of visualizing the journey as a ladder ascending only up to a predetermined height, the process is more accurately visualized as a **zigzag**, with points of clarity and detours; or a **spiral**, with points of clarity along with opportunities to reverse, revisit, revise, and refine. While not a "blueprint," given the uniqueness of each seeker, the creative process offers a generative guide for the journey, one that allows for—even expects and perhaps requires—departures, detours, mis-steps, and disappointments, experiences too-quickly and incorrectly disparaged as "failures" (Wadell and Pinches 110). Often, with reflection (through journaling, for example), the best learning arises from such zigzagging—an inherent part of the process, all part of the journey.

Finally, a journey to purpose is **lifelong**. That is, unlike engaging the creative process for a one-time, defined end—like creating a piece of art (see, for example, the account of creating *The Encounter* monument beginning on p. 12)—the journey to purpose is an ongoing, lifelong, creative act, one that requires re-engaging as the self continues to learn from all the being, doing, and reflecting. New insights arise. New directions can be taken. Purposes can be refined, re-attuned, to better match 'true self' and service (Burrow and Hill; Cahalan 2017).

It's Lasallian

An approach to a college education grounded in vocation and calling, and guided by the creative process, is an especially Lasallian approach to learning, working, and living, reflecting important aspects and values of the life of St. John Baptiste de La Salle, founder of the De La Salle Christian Brothers, as well as the ethos and aims of the Brothers and their lay partners as conducted today in 1,100 educational institutions in eighty countries.

De La Salle was poised to live a very privileged life as a priest with much family wealth, authority, and influence. However, he soon found himself called to a much different life for something more meaningful and other-directed: giving up his position, wealth, and institutional influence to teach and save impoverished children—both practically and spiritually—and forming an institute of Brothers that continues to exist more than three hundred years later. The book's epigraph (p. 2) emphasizes that De La Salle did not anticipate his vocation: It was "imperceptible...over a long period of time...one commitment led to another..."—reflecting a lifelong, faith-filled, creative process in support of meaningful service.

Your Turn

How might *you* begin to actively engage the creative process to cultivate your own journey to purpose? What will you discover about yourself and your unique gifts? What role will your communities play? What will be meaningful for you? How will you translate your meaningful insights and gifts into a contribution for others, lifelong, for a better world?

And how might these life stories from members of the Lewis community help illuminate your journey?

Works Cited

Buechner, Frederick. *Wishful Thinking: A Seeker's ABC*. Harper One, 1993. Clydesdale

Burrow, Anthony and Patrick Hill, eds. *The Ecology of Purposeful Living Across theLifespan: Developmental, Educational, and Social Perspectives*. Springer, 2020.

Cahalan, Kathleen A. and Bonnie J. Miller-McLemore, eds. *Calling All Years Good: Christian Vocation throughout Life's Seasons*. Wm. B. Eerdmans Publishing, 2017.

Cahalan, Kathleen A. and Douglas J. Schuurman, eds. *Calling in Today's World: Voicesfrom Eight Faith Perspectives*. Wm. B. Eerdmans Publishing, 2016.

Clydesdale, Tim. *Why Colleges Must Talk to Students about Vocation*. U of Chicago Press, 2015.

Csikszentmihalyi, Mihalyi. *Creativity: Flow and the Psychology of Discovery and Invention*. HarperCollins, 1996.

Dyk, B.J and R.D. Duffy. "Calling and Vocation at Work: Definitions and Prospects for Research and Practice." *The Counseling Psychologist*. 37(3) 2009, 424-450. https://doi.org/10.1177/0011000008316430.

NetVUE: The Network for Vocation in Undergraduate Education. https://cic.edu/networks/netvue/

Palmer, Parker. *Let Your Life Speak: Listening for the Voice of Vocation*. John Wiley &Sons, 2000.

Reyes, Patrick B. *The Purpose Gap: Empowering Communities of Color to Find Meaning and Thrive*. Westminster John Knox, 2021.

Sheldon, Kenneth M. *What the New Psychology of the Self Teaches Us About How to Live*. Basic Books, 2022.

Vedantam, Shankar (host). "Happiness 2.0: Cultivating Your Purpose." *Hidden Brain* podcast. *Hidden Brain Media*. https://hiddenbrain.org/podcast/cultivating-your-purpose/.

Vedantam, Shankar (host). "Who Do You Want to Be?" *Hidden Brain* podcast. *Hidden Brain Media*. https://hiddenbrain.org/podcast/what-do-you-want-to-be/.

Wadell, Paul J. and Charles R. Pinches. *Living Vocationally: The Journey of the Called Life*. Cascade Books, 2021.

Wapnick, Emilie. "Why Some of Us Don't Have One True Calling." TEDx, 2015. https://www.ted.com/talks/emilie_wapnick_why_some_of_us_don_t_have_one_true_calling?language=en

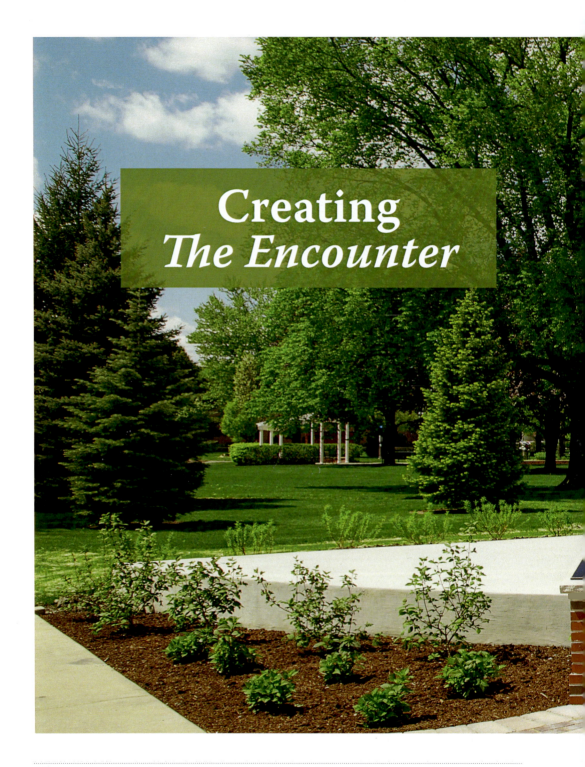

Creating
The Encounter

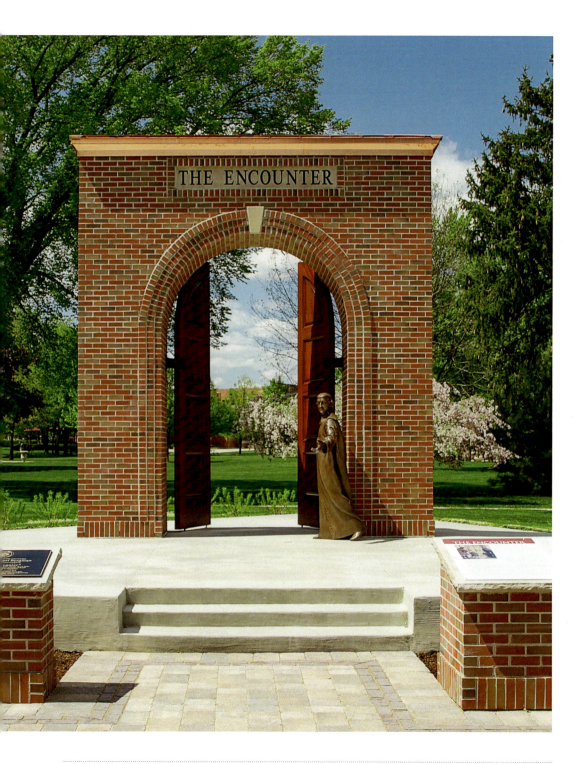

An *Encounter* Moment: From Reims to Romeoville

by **Kurt Schackmuth, Ph.D.**
Vice President for Student Life and Chief Mission Officer

Origins

The project was a creative, meaningful, and once-in-a-lifetime opportunity: A generous benefactor offered to fund the development and construction of an "iconic sculpture" on campus that would be attractive, unique, and reflective of the University's Mission and identity—a sculpture that would evoke a sense of emotion and appeal to current students and alumni alike.

Such iconic sculptures exist on campuses throughout the country and around the world, for example, the University of Notre Dame's *Grotto of Our Lady of Lourdes*; Michigan State University's storied "Sparty" statue; and Lorado Taft's *The Alma Mater* sculpture, a beloved symbol at the University of Illinois Urbana-Champaign that for over ninety years served as the backdrop for countless graduation photos. And now Lewis would be able to enjoy its own 'iconic sculpture.'

In August 2015, Brother James Gaffney, FSC, the University's President at the time, suggested the project to longtime friends and benefactors of Lewis University, Jay and Lori Bergman, who generously agreed to underwrite it. Brother James asked me to serve as project director and convene an especially creative group of faculty and staff to help imagine and articulate what the sculpture could be. The initial group included a Christian Brother, a theologian, an English professor, an artist, a historian, a fundraiser, and our superintendent of grounds; it gradually increased to include numerous other colleagues.

Brainstorming

Our "Iconic Sculpture Project" team, as we came to be known, approached the work in a holistic, comprehensive, and educational manner. We sought inspiration on other college campuses and in public squares and parks. We studied websites and photos of art pieces, sculptures, exhibits, memorials, and other places of symbolic meaning and historical significance. By October, we articulated the guiding principles for the project: The sculpture should reflect the Mission of the University, inspire a new campus tradition, center on an experience that one "enters into," and tell a meaningful story that unfolds as part of that experience.

Our conversation then turned towards themes for the sculpture itself—something that would make it truly 'iconic' for our community—such as aviation and flight; the identity of "The Flyer," the Lewis mascot;

the Lasallian star, and other ideas inspired by our Lasallian and Catholic Mission. There was also talk of plazas, amphitheaters, walls, benches, pavers, mosaics, pedestals, lighting, interpretative text panels, walkways, and more that would help us situate the sculpture in the appropriate setting. By mid-November, we were under pressure to present several viable options to the donors for their feedback and approval. And although we generated numerous ideas, we weren't yet unified around any one compelling option.

Conceptual Designs

In February 2016, after several additional months of brainstorming and discussion, we presented our "Iconic Sculpture Concepts" memorandum to the President and the donors for their consideration. Our proposal included three main concepts accompanied by images that inspired our thinking: the statue of an aviator that evoked our aviation heritage and the embodiment of 'The Flyer;' a large, stainless steel, five-pointed star evoking the Lasallian star and the University's Mission values; and a concept we called "Flight," a sculpture depicting an airplane with a long, flowing contrail meant to represent soaring, upward momentum.

By the early spring, we received helpful and constructive feedback from the donor expressing a preference for the project's focal point to represent an actual, iconic figure connected to the University rather than an abstract image or concept. Strong consideration was given to the possibility of memorializing Frank J. Lewis, one of the institution's founders and the University's

namesake. We invited Leslie Ansteth Colonna, Assistant Professor of Art and Design, to develop some sketches and watercolor concept images of Lewis standing alone in one depiction, and in another, accompanied by a high school-aged young man and a college-aged woman, both meant to represent Lewis's role in founding Holy Name Technical School and his legacy as the institution evolved into a university. We also sought out the expertise of Alec M. Smith, a St. Paul, Minnesota-based sculptor with whom the University had contracted for previous sculpture work. We also identified possible campus locations for the sculpture. Our overall concept was well-received, but many involved felt it didn't represent the energy and uniqueness we sought to evoke in the completed project. The timing was right for a pause, as Brother James Gaffney's presidency concluded that summer, and Dr. David Livingston was welcomed to campus as our tenth President.

New Energy and Inspiration

By October 2016, with a revitalized and reconstituted committee, I proposed that Saint John Baptist de La Salle serve as the central focal point of the project. I further suggested we envision a depiction of De La Salle that was unlike the traditional versions seen elsewhere. And so, we aimed to offer a decidedly "21st century" rendition of the Founder, one that would create a sense of pride, elicit emotion, and inspire. Most importantly, we wanted it to be an original— unique to Lewis and unlike anything seen elsewhere.

We quickly developed ideas around De La Salle as the central figure, discussing ways to represent the spirit, identity, meaning, and relatability of De La Salle to the viewer. We also considered how the sculpture might reflect the concepts of vocation and calling. Finally, we expressed a desire for the viewer or observer to interact with the statue.

And then we had a breakthrough moment! Our inspiration was "John Baptist de La Salle Meets Adrien Nyel," a painting from Gerlier's engraving in Gaveau's 1886 *Life of the Founder*. The painting depicts the events that occurred in March 1679, when twenty-seven-year-old John Baptist de La Salle visited the convent of the Sisters of the Child Jesus in Reims, France, to assist the Sisters with important business matters and to celebrate Mass. As he approached the doorway to the convent, De La Salle encountered Adrien Nyel and his fourteen-year-old teacher-assistant, Christophe. Nyel, a social services administrator, was from Rouen, where he had established schools for the poor. He had been asked by Madame Jeanne Dubois Maillefer, a wealthy widow, to consider founding a charity school for boys in Reims. Nyel's first visit in town was to seek guidance and support from the Sisters. Once inside the entryway to the convent, Sister Françoise Duval introduced the two men.

This chance encounter changed the trajectory of De La Salle's life. With each passing day, De La Salle found himself becoming drawn into an unfamiliar world, the world of the poor—a world of disadvantaged students, uncultured teachers, and families chronically oppressed by poverty. Although De La Salle didn't expect his involvement with Nyel and the schools to be a lasting project, he sensed that God was calling him to continue this important work. The rest, as they say, is history. In 1680, De La Salle went on to establish the Brothers of the Christian Schools.

Seeking the "Iconic"

What if we could capture this "encounter moment" in our depiction of De La Salle, yet also make that depiction relevant for a 21st century, college-going audience? How could we effectively interpret and communicate that 300-plus-year-old moment of discovery, promise, and impact in De La Salle's life for a new generation learning about the Founder and his educational mission? Before long, we were discussing not just a re-creation but a modern-day reinterpretation to inspire and teach others about this pivotal moment in the founding story of Lasallian education.

Soon, it all came together. Our sculpture of De La Salle would be positioned at the entry of an open doorway, hand outstretched, welcoming, inviting. We would communicate to the student that just as De La Salle's life changed from his encounter with Nyel, and opportunities presented themselves to him that he had not previously imagined before that day in March, the same could happen for all Lewis students. A Lasallian education could similarly open possibilities. A sense of purpose and calling could be discovered. Transformations could take place that one didn't expect. We agreed that we could design a ritual for new students around their passage through the doorway and that our initial hope of an "experience" could be realized by telling De La Salle's

> **"** What if we could capture this 'encounter moment' in our depiction of De La Salle, yet also make that depiction relevant for a 21st century, college-going audience? **"**

story, relating it to students today, and creating an engaging, interactive experience for students, alumni, and visitors. We finally discovered the 'iconic' concept we were seeking!

An Encounter Moment

Throughout 2017, we focused and executed. We presented our newest idea to Jay Bergman, and he enthusiastically approved. We studied De La Salle's "encounter moment" in more depth to better understand the circumstances around this crucial moment in the Lasallian story. Leslie Ansteth Colonna started sketching, painting, and sculpting a variety of conceptual images to help us develop and refine our ideas. We discussed important features like the size and scale of the sculpture and the "approachability factor:" We didn't want just observers; we wanted students and others to interact with the sculpture, to be able to walk up and directly approach De La Salle. We discussed at great length his stance, his facial expression, and the positioning of his arms and hands. Leslie invested countless hours bringing our ideas to life in drawn and painted form. Alec Smith was soon developing computer-generated, three-dimensional digital concept sculptures for us to marvel at and scrutinize in an effort to perfect our image of De La Salle. I consulted Brother

William Mann, FSC and Brother Gerard Rummery, FSC on De La Salle's appearance, his clothing, and even his height! We also spent time envisioning the doorway itself— its size, scale, shape, construction, and the positioning and location of De La Salle at the entrance to the doorway.

During the summer of 2018, we began working closely with architects and our Facilities staff on the necessary infrastructure for what we were now calling our "monument." We identified the ideal site at the center of campus, just off a main pedestrian thoroughfare, ensuring that the monument would be visible and familiar to all members of the Lewis community. Our Vice President for University Advancement helped managed the financial elements of the project and stayed connected with the Bergmans while I worked closely with Facilities, Leslie Ansteth Colonna, Alec Smith, and others to ensure that we were staying true to our overall concept plan.

By late 2018, the design work and architectural specifications and drawings were complete, materials were selected, and the concrete footings at the site had been poured by our contractor. From that point on, all the structural work for the project, save for a few finishing elements, were completed in-house by Lewis Facilities staff members, making the project even more meaningful. The brickwork construction of the doorway moved along swiftly despite cold and damp weather. The concrete deck surrounding the doorway was poured. Landscaping and plantings were installed. All that remained was the arrival of the Founder.

On April 26, 2019, a beautiful, sunny day, Alec Smith arrived from Minnesota with the sculpture of De La Salle. The sculpture was carefully wrapped and strapped to a pallet inside a box trailer attached to Alec's truck. With a forklift, Facilities staff carefully removed the pallet from the trailer. Alec then led a crew of four to carefully raise the 300-pound bronze sculpture of De La Salle onto the specially reinforced concrete, where anchors had been meticulously placed according to Alec's exacting specifications. Together, they moved the sculpture into position. Once De La Salle was secured in place, Alec and members of the Facilities team proudly posed for a photo, the first people to do so.

We scheduled the dedication ceremony for April 30, 2019, perfectly timed to coincide with the 368th anniversary of De La Salle's birth. Mother Nature, however, had other plans, and the ceremony was postponed due to heavy rain. Because we had arrived at the end of the academic year, we rescheduled the dedication for early in the fall semester.

Dedication and Blessing

After four years of ideation, discussions, strategizing, designing, refining, sculpting, and building, *The Encounter* was formally dedicated on the afternoon of Tuesday, September 24, 2019. Nearly a hundred faculty, staff, students, Trustees, Christian Brothers, alumni, and guests, including Jay and Lori Bergman, were in attendance for the formal dedication and blessing of the new monument. The ceremony became an occasion to share with the University community the meaning of *The Encounter* and what we hoped it could mean for students and others. In Brother Philip Johnson's blessing of the monument, he prayed, "It is our hope and prayer that as students arrive on campus they will encounter this sculpture, discover its symbolism, and commit themselves to being challenged: by new ideas, by people with different perspectives, by experiences that draw forth talents they may not have known they possessed, and by an openness to change and being changed."

Today, each August, as part the New Flyer Convocation, during which we tell De La Salle's encounter story and convey the significance of the monument, hundreds of first-year and transfer students pass through the doorway of *The Encounter*. This rite of passage begins with a procession from the Student Recreation and Fitness Center Fieldhouse to *The Encounter*, with faculty and staff lining the sidewalk and cheering the students as they approach De La Salle symbolically welcoming them into their Lasallian experience. The President, Provost, and members of the Christian Brothers community greet them on the other side of the doors, marking the official start of their Lewis experience.

▲ Celebrating *The Encounter* dedication on September 24, 2019 are (from left) Lewis University President Dr. David Livingston; artist and Lewis Art and Design Professor Leslie Ansteth Colonna; business leader Jay D. Bergman, whose generous support prompted the creating of *The Encounter*; sculptor Alec M. Smith; and Vice President for Mission Dr. Kurt Schackmuth. (Photograph by Joseph I. Glatz)

▲ From left, President Dr. David Livingston, monument donors Lori and Jay Bergman, and President Emeritus Br. James Gaffney, FSC. (Photograph by Joseph I. Glatz)

Inspirations

◀ **FIGURE 1A.** *John Baptist de La Salle Meets Adrien Nyel at the Convent of the Sisters of the Child Jesus, Rue du Barbâtre, Reims*. Circa 1679. Painting from Gerlier's engraving in Gaveau's 1886 *Life of the Founder*. (Retrieved from lasallianresources.org)

▲ **FIGURE 1B.** *Present Day Front Door at the Motherhouse of the Sisters of the Child Jesus, Reims, France*. (Retrieved from dlsfootsteps.org)

De La Salle's Encounter

The painting featured in Figure 1A is the only visual representation of the "encounter" that De La Salle experienced with Adrien Nyel, a lay person and educator who worked for many years in Rouen, France, establishing schools for the children of poor families. This encounter and their initial collaboration would change the course of De La Salle's life—his journey—and, in turn, the lives of countless others through his eventual founding of the Insititute of the Brothers of the Christian Schools.

Figure 1B is a current photograph of the convent door to the Motherhouse of the Sisters of the Child Jesus (also known as the Society of the Holy Child Jesus), a congregation established in 1670, located in Reims, France. Together, the doorway —the site of De La Salle's transformative encounter—the painting of that encounter (fig. 1A), and De La Salle's entire vocation journey serve as the inspiration for *The Encounter* monument.

From Inspiration to Visualization

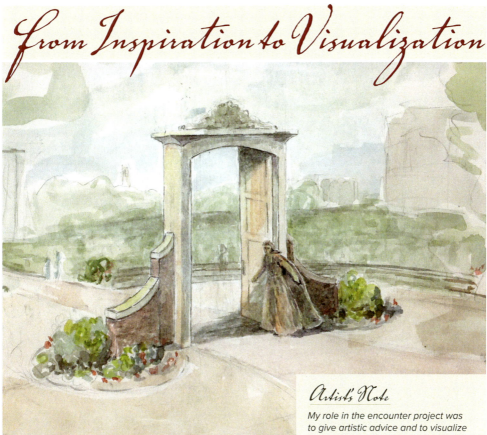

▲ **FIGURE 2A.** *Concept Illustration 1 of The Encounter Monument.* Leslie Ansteth Colonna. Graphite and watercolor on rag paper.

Situating and Sketching De La Salle

In an early sketch of the monument (fig. 2A), artist and Lewis Art and Design Professor Leslie Ansteth Colonna integrates the architectural motifs of the university's Learning Resource Center, including the flat roof and shape of the arches. This early version of the monument also includes winged walls and ornamentation above the archway, which were removed in later versions.

Artist's Note

My role in the encounter project was to give artistic advice and to visualize ideas as they developed through the collaborative committee process. The committee started by researching all sorts of successful public sculptures from various places, including civic plazas and other universities. This concept image came after many other sketches I did, including a large abstract five-point Lasallian star, an airplane propeller, and a portrait of Lewis' key founder and namesake Frank J. Lewis. The committee continually gravitated to a work that could tell De La Salle's story. This was the first sketch I did to include both a passageway and a statue of De La Salle. Once we settled on making De La Salle the essential part of the piece, my work then focused on designing a sculpture in the right setting to reflect all the ideas from the donor and the committee.

Artist's Note

To get as close as we could to a successful outcome, I created multiple sketches that explored various arrangements of the position and gesture of the De La Salle sculpture and the doorway, as well as to show where the monument might best be located on campus. I enjoyed my role visualizing and translating the committee's ideas into both aesthetic and practical visual solutions, using my expertise as an artist.

▲ **FIGURE 2B.** *Concept Image 2*. Leslie Ansteth Colonna. Graphite and mixed media on rag paper.

Artist's Note

Much of my work on these concept drawings included research on historical sculpture. The various poses reflect this. In this sketch, I put De La Salle in a different pose for the committee to consider. Here, De La Salle stands at the top of the steps with hands held out in front on him in a welcoming gesture. I also tried visualizing how a hexagonal platform might function.

▲ **FIGURE 2C.** *Concept Image 3*. Leslie Ansteth Colonna. Graphite and mixed media on rag paper.

In another early version of the monument (fig. 2B), the artist added doors, transforming the archway to a more clearly rendered doorway. De La Salle is shown ascending the stairs and ushering others towards the door. The stairs include the messaging: "Enter to Learn, Leave to Serve"— an adage and philosophy referenced in various Lasallian communities.

A later drawing (fig. 2C) reflects a more minimalist approach with a refined doorway structure, roofline, and stonework; the hexagon base was ultimately replaced with a rectangular base.

In another later drawing (fig. 2D), De La Salle is again shown forward of the doors (as in figs. 2B and 2C) but is now placed on a tiered pedestal. Both the pedestal and the placement of De La Salle relative to the doorway were reconsidered for a more accessible, inviting, and interactive aesthetic experience, more reflective of a Lasallian spirituality and ethos.

While the hexagonal base was later reconsidered, another later drawing (fig. 2E) reflects important decisive features: a more minimalist doorway structure, De La Salle positioned at the doorway with a welcoming gesture, and the monument's campus location at the southeast corner of the University Green near Sancta Alberta Chapel.

▲ **FIGURE 2D.** *Concept Image 4*. Leslie Ansteth Colonna. Graphite and mixed media on rag paper.

Artist's Note

I also researched every sculpture of De La Salle that I could find, from St. Peter's Basilica in Rome to high schools and universities worldwide. In this concept drawing, not only does this image (fig. 2D) show De La Salle on a pedestal, but the figure also appears larger than life. In the end, this composition did not represent the more accessible, inviting, and down-to-earth De La Salle we wished to convey—to create a monument that allowed for interaction and inspiration (fig. 2E).

▲ **FIGURE 2E.** *Concept Image 5*. Leslie Ansteth Colonna. Graphite and mixed media on rag paper.

Focusing

Artist's Note

While I considered this pose (fig. 3A) to be a welcoming gesture, in keeping with what the committee wanted, my husband, Lewis Theology Professor Dominic Colonna, noted that the pose is more one of prayer—an orans posture, a Latin term meaning one who is praying—which did not represent our intention for De La Salle's gesture.

▲ **FIGURE 3A.** *Close-up of De La Salle with Hands Extended*. Leslie Ansteth Colonna. Graphite on rag paper.

▶ **FIGURE 3B.** *Close-up of De La Salle at the Doorway*. Leslie Ansteth Colonna. Graphite and watercolor on rag paper.

Figuring De La Salle's Gesture

An early sketch of a close-up of De La Salle (fig. 3A), with his arms and hands extended in front of him, reflected an intention of a welcoming gesture, one that was later revised due to its theological understanding, as the artist discusses in her note.

A later sketch of De La Salle (fig. 3B), positioned at the threshold of the doorway with open arms and hands, reflects more closely the sought-after welcoming posture. Also included in this concept image—both reconsidered for the final version of the monument—are the Signum Fidei star on the door and, again, the inscribed message on the steps, "Enter to Learn, Leave to Serve," both of which were reconsidered for the final version.

◀ **FIGURE 3C.** *Clay Maquette of De La Salle*. Leslie Ansteth Colonna. 14" Clay.

In another early step in the process, artist Leslie Ansteth Colonna created a clay maquette (fig. 3C) to assist in articulating the most appropriate posture for De La Salle and the placement of his arms and hands.

from Concept to Realization

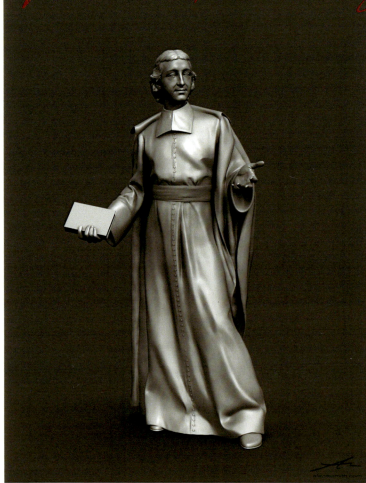

Artist's Note

In the initial model I submitted, I offered a pose which departed from quoting the Belvedere Apollo antique sculpture but which, I believe, captured a welcoming image of De La Salle when he met Nyel. I subsequently learned that this classical pose was the preferred and intended gesture, so I attempted to emulate its movement and grace for the second submission.

▲ **FIGURE 4A.** *Concept Model 1 for De La Salle Bronze Sculpture*.
Alec M. Smith. Digital sculpture rendering.

Digital Renderings and Bronze Sculpture

Figure 4A is sculptor Alec Smith's first gestural interpretation—i.e., De La Salle's stance and position of his hands—of artist Leslie Ansteth Colonna's illustrations and clay maquette, rendered into a 3D digital sculpture.

▲ **FIGURE 4B.** *Concept Model 2 for De La Salle Bronze Sculpture*.
Alec M. Smith. Digital sculpture rendering.

The sculptor's second gestural interpretation (fig. 4B) shows De La Salle moving forward while simultaneously looking to and inviting those he's encountering.

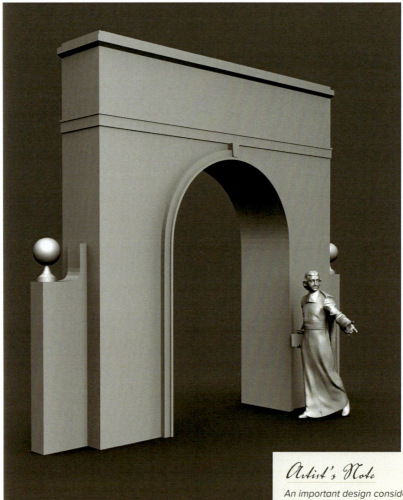

▲ **FIGURE 4B2.** *Concept Model 2 for De La Salle Bronze Sculpture with Archway*. Alec M. Smith. Digital sculpture rendering.

Artist's Note

An important design consideration in sculpture is how the piece will occupy space in the installation setting. Simulating the sculpture standing next to the archway can help affirm the design or make clear any changes that should be made. Also, for all the digital renderings, I relied on a software called Zbrush to digitally sculpt the model for the De La Salle sculpture. The STL file created—a file format commonly used for 3D printing and computer-aided design (CAD)—can be used to create rendered illustration in software packages like Keyshot and Photoshop. The file is also used to CNC mill the internal foam armature (see fig. 4C)—a computerized milling process known as Computer Numerical Control.

Figure 4B2 is a digital rendering of the sculptural model of De La Salle placed next to a concept archway, allowing the sculptor to test the placement and gesture of the finished sculpture.

Artist's Note

At this stage, using traditional methods of sculpture, the sculptor can reassess the design of the sculpture at full size. This is an important step because being in front of the sculpture in person is a more resonant, sensory experience than viewing the model on the computer screen.

Artist's Note

Depending on the design of the sculpture, it can be convenient to work on areas as separated pieces. Having pieces separated can also be convenient for delivery to the foundry, the factory for casting metal. Many times, the foundry will separate these pieces for molding. After being cast in bronze, the pieces are then welded together.

Figure 4C is an image of the armature, or support structure, for the application of modeling clay, which is modeled to achieve the detail required for the final bronze sculpture. The file for the digital concept model (fig. 4B2) is used by a fabricator to carve an internal armature for the life-sized clay model of the De La Salle sculpture.

Figure 4D reflects a focus on De La Salle's left arm—a key feature of the sculpture contributing to De La Salle's welcoming gesture—separated from the figure. Working on the separated left arm, the sculptor is able to turn the piece over and view the work from several different angles.

Artist's Note

The wax pattern stage is the phase where the sculptor can change details on the sculpture or make final touch-ups before sending it to the foundry to be cast in bronze.

▲ **FIGURE 4E.** *Life-Sized Cast Wax Pattern*. Alec M. Smith. Digital photo.

Figure 4E captures the wax pattern stage, the next intricate step in the traditional and highest quality process of transforming De La Salle's model into a finished sculpture. To achieve this, a mold is created from the life-sized clay sculpture, and hollow wax positives are cast from the mold. These positive wax patterns will be encased in a ceramic shell called investment. The wax is melted out of the investment, and molten bronze is poured in, which fills the area that the wax patterns had once occupied. The investment, or ceramic shell, is then broken off revealing the bronze sculpture, in parts which will then be welded together, ground down, sanded, and polished into its finished form.

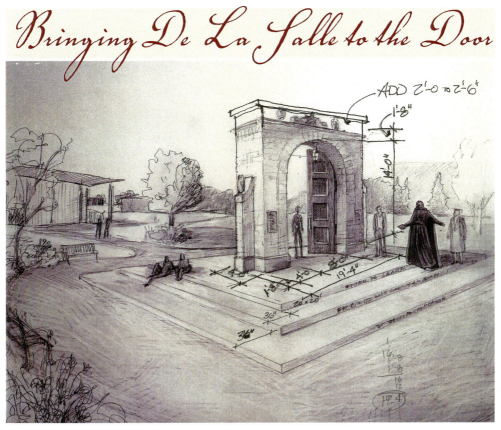

Bringing De La Salle to the Door

▲ **FIGURE 5A.** *De La Salle Art and Sculpture Project*. Tom Roth. Green and Associates. Architectural drawing.

Building and Installing

Figures 5A and 5B show an in-process architectural drawing of the monument reflecting several refinements to the work—e.g., eliminating the metal roof, replacing cast stone and lime stone with brick, and removing the winged walls, decorative scrolls, and star. This refining process—necessitated, in part, by the budget, and a typical feature of the creative process—helped to clarify the form, realize its essence, ultimately creating a simplicity and unity in both form and spirit. "A grace moment," noted Bother Philip Johnson, FSC, Coordinator of Special Projects for Mission, and a member of the committee.

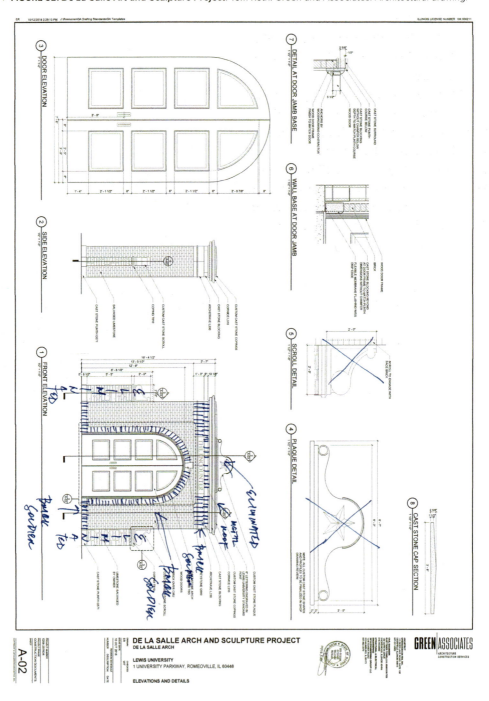

Figure 6A shows a member of the university's Facilities department laying the bricks and creating the foundation for the monument.

After arriving on campus with the sculpture in tow from his studio in Minnesota, the sculptor Alec M. Smith and several members of the university's Facilities department, led by the university's Associate Vice-President of Facilities Keith Kameron, are shown (fig. 6B) working in sync as they install the sculpture of De La Salle at the doorway.

FIGURE 6A. *Building the Setting*. Photograph. Margaret Martinez

▲ FIGURE 6B. *Installation of De La Salle with Sculptor Alec M. Smith and Members of University Facilities. Photograph. Margaret Martinez.*

The Encounter in Action

A New Tradition is Born

The Encounter offers an opportunity for students and the entire university community to more fully experience De La Salle's vocation journey and, in turn, more intentionally begin or renew their own journey to purpose. During the university's annual First-Year Convocation, first-year students, accompanied by faculty and staff, form a procession to the monument where they are met by De La Salle's welcoming invitation to walk through the door to their own encounters, vocations, and callings.

At Commencement, students are once again invited to walk back through the door, to signal their readiness to continue their journey—contributing their learning and gifts to the world. *The Encounter* makes possible these nourishing community rituals, commemorating both De La Salle's vocation journey and the living legacy of the Institute of the Brothers of the Christian Schools, helping to cultivate the vocations and callings of young people and communities worldwide.

▲ FIGURE 8A. *Artist and Lewis Professor of Art and Design Leslie Ansteth Colonna*.

▲ FIGURE 8B. *Sculptor Alec M. Smith.*

Reflections on the Journey from St. John Baptist de La Salle

Adapted from *The Memoir on the Beginnings*, 1721

A few years after his encounter with Adrian Nyel and his involvement in organizing and training the first teachers, St. La Salle's spiritual director asked him to reflect on this period of his life. In part, he wrote:

I had thought that the care which I took of the schools and of the teachers would only be external, something which would not involve me any further than to provide for their subsistence and to see to it that they carried out their duties with piety and assiduity.

... It was by these two events, namely by my meeting Monsieur Nyel and by the proposal made to me by Madame Maillefer, that I began to take an interest in the schools for boys. Prior to this, I had never given them a thought.

... Indeed, if I had ever thought that the care I was taking of the schoolmasters out of pure charity would ever have made it my duty to live with them, I would have dropped the whole project. For since, naturally speaking, I considered the men whom I was obliged to employ in the schools at the beginning as being inferior to my valet,

the mere thought that I would have to live with them would have been insupportable to me. In fact, I experienced a great deal of unpleasantness when I first had them come to my house. This lasted two years.

It was undoubtedly for this reason that God, who guides all things with wisdom and serenity, whose way it is not to force the inclinations of persons, willed to commit me entirely to the development of the schools. God did this in an imperceptible way and over a long period of time, so that one commitment led to another in a way I did not foresee in the beginning.

De La Salle embraced unexpected invitations in his life, met challenging experiences that expanded his perspective and gifts, and discovered new meaning and purpose in his life. How receptive are you to exploring unforeseen opportunities throughout your collegiate journey? Are you open to being pleasantly—and unpleasantly—surprised by new insights? As a member of the Lewis community, how will you actively pursue personal growth and educational possibilities?

Radical Space of Possibility: Creating Spaces of Healing, Creating Spaces of Wholeness

by Tennille Nicole Allen, Ph.D.

Professor and Chair, Department of Sociology
Program Director of African American Studies and Ethnic and Cultural Studies

Are you sure, sweetheart, that you want to be well? ... Just so's you're sure, sweetheart, and ready to be healed, cause wholeness is no trifling matter. A lot of weight when you're well. —Toni Cade Bambara, *The Salt Eaters*

These words from Bambara's work of Black woman genius are uttered by Minnie Ransom—described in the novel as the "fabled healer of the district." Minnie poses these words to the book's protagonist, Velma Henry, a Black feminist activist who had just attempted suicide, before they commenced with the work of Velma's healing. In this powerful passage, Bambara captures the notion that for African American women, there is tremendous power, possibility, and responsibility contained within the decision to heal and achieve wholeness. She also notes the interconnectedness and agency found within being healed and being whole. Through this interconnectedness and agency, practices of remembering and reclamation are recalled in order to facilitate someone who is on a path to come into balance, into healing, and back into herself. These words of remembering and reclamation also are an invocation, both for Velma and for me, an African American woman academic. Though my realities are different from Velma's fictional world, the questions of healing, wholeness, and wellness are no trifling matter for me. They indeed invoke a call that needs a response, one that, in turn, calls on the transformative traditions they evoke to enter spaces of healing and greater wholeness.

One question and call I am seeking to answer has involved the transformative potential for healing and wholeness through my beliefs, approaches, and practices around my teaching. Much like other African American women in the academy,

I face hostility, isolation, and devaluation through my being Black and woman in what has been and what remains a predominantly White and male space. Though I could, I do not write here about those numerous microaggressions or the recurrent macroaggressions from students, staff, and faculty that I experience. Instead, I am affirming Minnie Ransom's notion of healing to center a practice that carves out and protects spaces for healing and wholeness outside and despite these realities. The classroom—my classroom—is a particularly critical place to do this in.

Like many other academics, my approach to teaching is one that urges student engagement and agency during the course—and hopefully well after the class ends. Much like political philosopher Joy James, my pedagogy allows students to actively link their individual lives with larger contexts and forces as they employ critical thinking and see themselves as creators of knowledge. This transformative process happens as they conduct research that is used by community partners, including local churches, afterschool programs, food banks, and labor organizers–research that not only helps document the challenges, joys, strengths, needs, and assets in local communities but also helps these organizations call for and create change. In my classrooms, I marry a Black feminist pedagogy with the sociological imagination as we interrogate social life at individual, interactional, institutional levels as it intersects, reflects, impacts, and transmutes within multiple spaces and forms. Patricia Coleman-Burns describes this as a "pedagogy of transformation to liberate, transform, and revolutionize people" (141). Such a pedagogy extends beyond the physical boundaries of the classroom.

Students in my courses do public sociology: They engage in community-based participatory research, advocacy, letter-writing and media campaigns, tweeting, as well as public actions on campus, such as teach-ins, film screenings and discussions, and conference presentations. It is important that students in my classes and department see ways that sociology can inform not just the projects that they do in their courses but through the course of their careers. Many of my students aspire to careers in the helping professions—social work, advocacy, education, counseling, occupational therapy, and the like. As most of my students are straight, White students, their straight, White, familial community, educational, and cultural contexts mean that the African American, Latinx, and/or LGBTQ+, and other marginalized people they will work with in these professions have been the Other they have learned to problematize, pity, or fear. Once I realized this, it became an imperative that I shift these students' lenses in my work with them in the classroom. When working with and within community contexts, I teach students from a perspective aimed to disrupt the prejudices and stereotypes that populate their worldviews by emphasizing

·

communities' and their residents' rich abilities, capacities, knowledge, and other existing resources. This disruptive practice and emphasis on community agency are an extension of the Black feminist pedagogy that I practice.

Another dimension of the Black feminist pedagogy that I practice is bringing my whole self to the classroom. As a professor and an African American woman, I am acutely aware of the need to create places of refuge, community, and support to withstand and address the difficulty that those of us who embody marginalized identities endure as we move through oppressive environs where we are often tolerated at best, viewed with skepticism most often, and have hostility and violence visited upon us far too frequently. My sociology classrooms reflect these places of refuge, community, and support when I show up as a Black woman, offer examples that center Black experiences, and collaborate with nonprofit organizations in Black communities to design class projects that serve these local organizations. The readings that I choose, the assignments and projects that I design, and the classroom communities that students and I co-create within the classroom are designed to lay bare the intricacies of individuals, ideologies, and institutions that oppress and repress in the service of transformation and justice. The creation of such spaces and the use of such pedagogy require fortitude. These all require the cultivation of openness to work through and past resistance. It is within

these spaces that a classroom community where recognizing and dismantling systems of oppression can occur. Through and in this space, the classroom can support healing and wholeness in multiple ways. This means that the classroom I seek to create is not a comfortable one—for me or for students.

Students do not automatically embrace my pedagogy. I am explicit in my classroom objectives, which are stated in the syllabus, embedded in readings and assignments, and reiterated verbally. Still, there are students along political and other identity affiliations who balk. Some students, especially those who would enroll in a general education class, drop or avoid my classes altogether. Of those students who do enroll in my courses, I am certainly most encouraged by those who take multiple classes with me, decide to major in sociology, and write and speak of the questions and answers that the sociology courses they have with me have provided them. Those others, however, in some ways push my pedagogical transformations the most. These students include those who discuss being made to feel guilty. For those students, I encourage them to reject feelings of guilt and contemplate actions to mitigate whatever inequalities have animated their guilt. I remind these students that feeling guilty is a luxury they can ill afford if they want to truly affect change. For other students, particularly those who come from marginalized communities, feelings of anger and powerlessness arise sometimes. I remind these students that anger can be transformative (Lorde 1984) and that they

> The readings that I choose, the assignments and projects that I design, and the classroom communities that students and I co-create...are designed to lay bare the intricacies of individuals, ideologies, and institutions that oppress and repress in the service of transformation and justice.

have and can exercise agency. I structure my courses to ensure that as we delve into the systemic, interlocking inequalities that undergird all that forms the United States, we also explore that these systemic, interlocking inequalities have been rejected and resisted by those who would experience these since before the nation's founding.

No matter their identities and ideologies, I acknowledge and welcome my students' frustrations with the issues around racism, sexism, homophobia, imperialism, ableism, and the other forms of oppression we analyze in class. I tell them of my frustrations with these systems and inform them that we should all feel these frustrations, and just as sitting in an uncomfortable position at our desks is solved by moving around until we are better positioned, we can use sociological theories, methods, and data to move thinking, practices, policies, laws, and the like until those of us who are subordinated are similarly better positioned. These transformations are certainly related to and rooted in my desire to create spaces reflective of commitment, culture, and community that facilitate healing and wholeness within these spaces and for students. The fight

for justice has never been a safe one. The work is inherently risky, and while these risks are political, they also are personal. bell hooks notes the personal nature of the risk as she states those of us employing this form of teaching have to both "be actively committed to a process of self-actualization that promotes their own well-being if they are to teach in a manner that empowers students" (15) and "accept the chaos and emotion that can occur when disrupting students' worldviews" (247). When we do, we can find that we have created spaces of healing and transformation personally and pedagogically.

Much of my time as a professor has also been spent reconciling my training from Northwestern University where I was trained to focus on research by some of the most brilliant and prolific scholars who were my professors, mentors, and friends. The mold I was expected to fit within diverged significantly from my new reality at an institution where teaching is the focus and scholarship is defined much broader than my training that focused almost exclusively on publishing highly acclaimed books or within the most prestigious journals suggested was possible. Questions of belonging and scholarly identity have been with me since accepting this position. While I am fortunate to have found employment and subsequent tenure and promotion in an institution that recognizes my work in the classroom, on campus, and in the community, through this process I have had to recalibrate my personal sense of scholarly success and fulfillment, and doing community-based participatory research (CBPR) is key to this.

In its grounding in community-identified, action-oriented research priorities, CBPR weds my teaching with my scholarship to ease this tension that I struggle against to publish research that matters. CPBR has made me recalibrate my definition of "research that matters" as I now believe that conducting research that is recognized and used by residents of places I care about makes more of a difference than acclaim and citation by other sociologists. I have made a number of connections with community organizations that influence my teaching and research in revitalizing ways that create spaces of wholeness and healing for my professional identity that resonate with my desire to use my position in service of African American people and communities. One area that I have been able to do this is in my interest in food justice. I have partnered with an organization near campus, headed by an African American woman, in research and other work on urban agriculture and a related youth-led social enterprise. Our efforts, which often involve my students

as researchers and through coursework projects, focus on sustainability, various measures of well-being, and the provision of food and economic opportunities in a community lacking in options for either. In this work, I have not only helped to repair disconnections between myself as a scholar and a teacher but also between my academic home and a disinvested Black community that can benefit from the resources and knowledge they have identified as important for them.

I began another CBPR project at this site in November 2016, at the request of the executive director who has worked for decades focusing much of her efforts and attention on African American boys—that is, until she, in keeping with others around the nation (Crenshaw, Ocen, and Nanda 2015; Morris 2015), noticed the perils that she worried about for her boys were also faced by African American girls. To rectify this, she asked if I would work with African American girls enrolled in an afterschool program she runs. I jumped at the chance to meet with them weekly to learn and dialogue about critical media literacy, Black feminist thought, identity, relationships, the arts, and how they create and recognize joy within their lives. Our work, designed collaboratively by the executive director, the girls, and me to address the disappearing and invisibilization of African American girls' experiences, needs, and concerns, also addresses what I had feared would be my disappearing and invisible identity as a researcher. This work offers another opportunity for the creation of healing and wholeness for me and the communities I am connected to through community-engaged and community-defined sociological research and practice.

As a Black feminist sociologist, through my lived-experience and academic knowledge, I am well aware of systematic oppressions created through centuries of ideologies, institutions, and structures that we were not meant to survive. I am also aware of the power of agency and a culture of resistance that struggles against, around, and through these systems. It is with this awareness that I enter the struggle, emphasizing my concern with the cultivation of spaces where commitment, culture, and community are invoked such that resistance and restoration, healing and wholeness can occur. In these ways, I can see the potential for transformation in my sociological practice and pedagogy and know they foster what is "a radical space of possibility" (hooks 12).

Works Cited

Bambara, Toni Cade. *The Salt Eaters.* New York: Vintage, 1980.

Coleman-Burns, Patricia. "'The Revolution Within: Transforming Ourselves." *Spirit, Space and Survival: African American Women in (White) Academe*, edited by Joy James and Ruth Farmer. New York: Routledge, 1993, pp. 139-157.

hooks, bell. *Teaching to Transgress: Education as the Practice of Freedom.* New York: Routledge, 1994.

James, Joy. "Teaching Theory, Talking Community." *Spirit, Space and Survival: African American Women in (White) Academe*, edited by Joy James and Ruth Farmer. New York: Routledge, 1993, pp. 118-135.

Lorde, Audre. *Sister Outsider.* Trumansburg, NY: Crossing Press, 1984.

Drifting to a Definition of Self and Calling

by Bonnie Bondavalli, Ph.D., J.D.

Former Dean of the College of Arts and Sciences
Dean of the College of Education and Social Sciences (Retired)

At various points in my life, I've been asked questions like, "How did you decide to go to college, select a school, or pick a major?" "How did you plan your career?" "Why did you choose Lewis?" My problem in responding is that words like *decide, select, pick, plan*, and *choose* don't really apply to the most significant events and turning points in my life. If I'm honest about it, my definition of myself, what I see as my strengths and weaknesses, and my purpose are largely due to events and people in my life. I think the word *drift* better describes how my life progressed from one place to another. I moved with the flow, was urged along by outside forces, and was blessed by wonderful people who propelled me in different directions.

First, I wouldn't even exist if there hadn't been some major events in my parents' lives that brought them together. My dad grew up on a farm in Nebraska and my mom on a farm in South Dakota. When they were young, both states suffered from severe drought in the "Dust Bowl" and swarms of grasshoppers so thick they sometimes blocked out the sun and left fields bare. My dad was eighteen and my mom ten when the stock market crashed in 1929 and the Great Depression began. My dad's father died when he was six, and my dad was the oldest of four children raised by a single mother, so there wasn't much money even before the Depression. To reduce the financial burden on the family, like many young men at the time, my father became a "hobo"— "riding the rails" looking for work. As conditions started to improve in parts of the Great Plains, South Dakota needed "farm hands," and my mom's hometown also had jobs in the quarries, so my dad ended up in Milbank working at Dakota Granite and helping local farmers. When World War II began, he was drafted.

While overseas, my dad wrote, and eventually proposed, to that "nice girl" he met in Milbank. (I was able to read his war-time letters because my mom saved them all.) Before World War II ended, though, my mother's parents gave up on South Dakota and moved to Sterling, Illinois, which was known for industry. Many factories, including Northwestern Steel & Wire—one of the biggest steel mills in the country—lined (and polluted) the Rock River, which ran between Sterling and Rock Falls. When he was discharged, my dad went to Sterling, married my mom, and took a job at Frantz Manufacturing where my grandfather worked. I was born in 1946. My mom worked in a grocery store; my grandmother worked in a department store. Grandma and Grandpa had twenty-two grandchildren. I had no siblings but a total of thirty-three first cousins.

The earliest major turning point in my own life was first grade. Measles, mumps, and chickenpox were common illnesses of childhood, and I got all three in one year. I also had my tonsils removed and got hit by a car. I spent most of first grade on a rollaway bed in the living room, sleeping, crying, or watching our 12-inch TV—which was super special because it included a record player and radio. But there wasn't much children's educational programming then, and neither of my parents had ever heard of "home schooling." My dad never went to high school, and my mom went for only two years. So, I didn't get much education that year and fell way behind my classmates. I was healthy in second and third grade but never did as well as other students. My

teachers didn't seem to expect much of me, and everyone, including me, accepted the idea that I just wasn't very bright.

Then we moved across the river to Rock Falls. In sixth grade, the fifth and sixth grade classes were large but not large enough to split into two of each, so they put the top one-third of each grade in a combined class, and, amazingly, I was assigned to that class. Everyone was back together in one seventh grade, and we had a young teacher with a novel idea I'm pretty sure no professional educator today would endorse: Each grading period, he put students in order by grades—highest grades in the row by the windows and lowest in the row by the door. I spent the whole year in the front seat of the row by the windows, so even if it wasn't good pedagogy, his plan profoundly changed my view of myself. I also appreciated that he assigned students with higher grades to mentor students with lower grades. At eighth grade graduation, I received the American Legion Award. My dad was so proud. Going into high school, I was confident that I could learn, and, when we graduated, I was salutatorian.

In high school, our English teacher took my best friend and me to Normal to visit his alma mater, Illinois State University (ISU). No one in my family or my friend's family had gone to college, so that was our only college visit, and we became roommates at ISU. I studied to be a teacher because ISU was known for teacher education and because my high school advisor told me that my GPA gave me choices. He listed nurse, teacher, and secretary. I preferred teacher. My family could afford the tuition—it was relatively low then—and I also received an Illinois State Teacher's Scholarship, established in response to a national teacher shortage.

I was a secondary education social studies major, and I worked in the library. The library was a good place for me because although I was now confident I could get good grades, I was shy—shy enough that the class I dreaded most was Speech. I didn't mind researching a topic but definitely did not want to stand in the front of the room and talk about it. After one of my speeches, the professor repeatedly told me that I should not "hide my light under a bushel." I didn't know what that meant but discovered the phrase came from a parable referenced in the Gospels of Matthew, Mark, and Luke. Apparently, the teacher was telling me I had a gift that shouldn't be put in a container or under a bed. It should be on display so others could see it. That was an astounding thought. I didn't and still don't entirely accept the idea, but I began to recognize that education was providing me great gifts, and I had an obligation to use them wisely.

As a social science student, I studied history, political science, economics, sociology, and psychology. I was fascinated by each of these disciplines. Their research provides insights into past and current events, and, if we take them seriously, each can help build a better and safer future. Sociology, however, seemed to bring all these fields of study together. Sociologists help us identify norms, values, traditions, and beliefs that shape and are shaped by organizations, communities, and nations. They are interested in how an individual's economic and social status, education, race, ethnicity, sexual orientation, and experiences affect perceptions. Sociology helped me recognize how I fit into the world around me and helped me comprehend, at least a little better, the dramatic political and cultural events happening when I was in high school and college. That turbulent time included the Vietnam War and anti-war protests; the Cuban Missile Crisis; civil rights protests and the Civil Rights Act; the Equal Pay Amendment; the Fair Housing Act; the assassinations of President John Kennedy, Dr. Martin Luther King, Jr., Malcolm X, and Robert Kennedy; Kent State; the Stonewall Inn uprising; the Woodstock Rock Festival; the increased popularity of drugs like marijuana and LSD; and the beginnings of the War on Drugs.

When my undergraduate advisor realized I could graduate in three and a half years, he convinced me to start working on a master's in sociology and arranged for a graduate assistantship. I spent the spring semester at ISU, and then, with encouragement from my advisor, I transferred to an affordable university that offered both the M.A. and Ph.D. in sociology—the University of Missouri (or Mizzou). Not surprisingly, given the events at that time related to crime, inequality, landmark legislation, and Supreme Court decisions, I chose to concentrate on

> **"**
>
> As we move through life, doors of opportunity are opened or closed for us, but that doesn't mean we have no control over our own futures. We need to recognize opened doors and doors we need to push to open fully, and we need to accept that we can't open every door.
>
> **"**

sociology of law and criminology. I was awarded a National Defense Education Act fellowship, established earlier when the Soviet Union launched Sputnik, the world's first satellite, and Congress feared that education in the USSR was superior to education in the United States.

The first semester at Mizzou, I was in a math stats course with students in several graduate programs. An international student—I wasn't sure where he was from—walked with me back to the sociology building a few times and took me to lunch once. We didn't seem to hit it off, and I didn't see him after we completed the course—until one Saturday night when I went to the library to get away from a guinea pig party (really) that my roommate, her boyfriend, some friends, and their guinea pigs were having in our apartment. When the library closed, I looked around to see if I knew anyone I could spend a little time with, so I'd be sure the party was over before I got home. The only person I knew was Bruno, the international student from statistics. We "happened" to leave at the same time, talked, and went for a long walk. I learned he was from Italy, but his mother, like many Italians, had moved to South America looking for a

better life. He joined her in Venezuela when he was fourteen. She had arranged a job for him, and with the guidance of new friends, he was able to go to night high school. He took a mechanical drafting class, and his teacher, who worked for Exxon Mobil, got him a job there. He saved money, came to the United States to study, and was working on a master's in agricultural economics. A few days later, he introduced me to two friends from Cambodia and Greece—who would become best man and groomsman at our wedding.

Bruno, the kindest, most patient, thoughtful person I know, "put the stamps in my passport" (as Sandra Bullock's character said in one of my favorite romantic comedies, *While You Were Sleeping*). Our honeymoon was the first of many trips to Italy, and I—a woman from the Midwest, and whose great-grandparents came from Norway, Poland, Germany, and Austria—became an Italian citizen. I love the name Bondavalli—meaning "good people from the valley"—the culture of that valley, particularly Bruno's hometown of Reggio Emilia, and the local food, like Parmigiano-Reggiano and prosciutto. After we honeymooned in Italy, Bruno and I moved to Venezuela, where I became a legal resident and taught English as a foreign language at Universidad de Carabobo.

I had finished all but the dissertation for the Ph.D. and made a trip back to the United States to do some research. During that trip, I went to an American Sociological Association conference. Some sociology professors from ISU were there. I still don't know how it happened. I didn't know they had an opening, and I didn't apply, but they offered me an assistant professor position. I thought that was unworkable, and back in Venezuela on another walk with Bruno, who now had a good job with International Multifoods Corporation, I told him about the offer. He said it could be a great opportunity and that I should consider it. He'd stay in Venezuela, and I'd move to Normal for an exploratory year. Then we'd decide which country was best for us.

As unrealistic as that sounds now, especially since we were expecting a baby, I took the job. Our daughter Teresa was born ten days before classes began. During the week, my mom stayed with Teresa and me in a tiny apartment in Normal; and on weekends, we made the 125-mile trip to my parents' home in Rock Falls, where I planned classes, and my mother washed clothes and made frozen dinners for my father. The next year, my mom returned to Rock Falls, and Bruno's mom, who spoke no English, joined us, and our principal household language became Spanish.

It took Bruno a long time to get authorization to work, residency status, and eventually his third citizenship in the U.S. Since he could not legally work for anyone else, he put savings into an imported bicycle shop which he ran until we moved to a little town between Normal and Champaign–Urbana, so he could study for his doctorate in bilingual education at the University of Illinois. While researching his dissertation in Chicago, Bruno met Fr. Carlos Plazas, Ph.D., and they ended up collaborating, with support from Spanish Episcopal Services and others, to establish St. Augustine College—the first bilingual institution of higher education in the Midwest. Our son Daniel was born during finals week of my last year at ISU, and we moved to Downers Grove. Bruno became Dean of the Faculty at St. Augustine, and I was fortunate to find a faculty position at a religiously affiliated, mission-focused, private university. I continued to enjoy teaching and interacting with students, helping them better understand and think critically about social issues and encouraging them so see the world from other people's perspectives. I was also involved in the operation of the university, serving on many committees, chairing the Sociology and Social Work Department, and serving as the first chair of the faculty senate.

I remained fascinated with sociology of law, criminology, and criminal justice and occasionally told Bruno I wished I had gone to law school. (When I was in college, the percent of female law students was in the single digits.) Finally, Bruno said, "Go take the Law School Admission Test, apply, and see what happens." I received a scholarship from John Marshall Law School (which offered an evening program), continued teaching, and graduated *magna cum laude*. During an extended year-and-a-half sabbatical, I worked as an attorney with the Office of State Appellate Defender representing indigent—almost all incarcerated—juvenile and adult clients, but I loved teaching and wanted to share what I'd learned with students. I was awarded the title "Distinguished Professor" and went on to serve as Dean of the College of Arts and Sciences. Several years later, however, I began to question whether my university, which I respected and continue to care about, was the place I could contribute the most. Bruno insisted that I explore alternatives.

In 2004, I became Associate Dean of the College of Arts and Sciences at Lewis, a Catholic and Lasallian university whose values of Fidelity, Wisdom, Knowledge, Justice, and Association spoke to my life and the sense of purpose my experiences and the people in my life had fostered. I had the privilege of serving as Dean of Arts and Sciences from 2009 to 2019, and, when the colleges were restructured, I became Dean of the College of Education and Social Sciences. Lewis and its extraordinary faculty, staff, administrators, and students provided me an opportunity to move whatever light I have from under a bushel, and I am deeply grateful.

In July of 2020, after almost fifty years in higher education, I retired and didn't have the opportunity to spend—except remotely, of course—my final months with the wonderful colleagues I had learned to love, and I wasn't able to pass out diplomas to the graduating students we all strive to serve. In that difficult year, we all experienced a devastating new event—a pandemic—and I wonder how COVID-19 will change the rest of my life, my children's lives, our community, our culture, the world. I also can't help but compare the polarization and protests in 2020 to the civil unrest and demonstrations in response to inequality in education, housing, health care, employment, and criminal justice in the 1960s and '70s that so influenced me as a person and produced positive but inadequate changes in law and policy. Will we be able to mend our political divides, improve police practices, implement fair and humane immigration policies, reduce educational and income inequality, and provide for the public health? And how will the journey through this time influence the futures of all those who experience it?

Reflecting on my life, I've learned through experience and through sociology that how we see ourselves, view possibilities, define our purpose and future, and even deal with adversity are dependent in significant part on events and people that we can't predict or control. National and international events—like a drought, depression, war, pandemic, or a social movement; personal experiences, like an illness, a loss, a chance meeting; or input from a teacher/mentor, family member, or friend—can limit options or provide unexpected opportunities. As we move through life, doors of opportunity are opened or closed for us, but that doesn't mean we have no control over our own futures. We need to recognize opened doors and doors we need to push to open fully, and we need to accept that we can't open every door. We need to devote time, energy, and commitment to the opportunities that we do accept.

Personally, I drifted through much of my life. Opportunities came to me more often than I sought them out, but along the way, I developed what sociologists would label a "self." I also discovered what others term a "calling" or "callings." As a Lutheran, I grew up hearing about Martin Luther's view of God's calling as more than a call to church work or even to career but to all the roles in our lives—professional and personal. I have valued my callings throughout life, and, in retirement, it will remain my goal to share the gifts I have received through my continuing roles as spouse, parent, friend, citizen, hopefully grandparent, and maybe, to a more limited extent than in the past, teacher or lawyer. For as long as God allows, I will strive to achieve the Lewis mission goals that became my own.

The Challenge is Sometimes the Opportunity

by Jennifer Buss, Ph.D.

Associate Professor, Department of Education
Special/Combined Education Program

From an early age, we ask our children what they want to be when they grow up. Some of these answers may range from being a princess, doctor, teacher, scientist, or firefighter. This simple question influences our lives and causes us to model the types of people that we look up to. From this question, I was asked to look at myself and answer not only *what* I wanted to be, but more importantly *who* I wanted to be. I wanted to be someone who made a difference, a person that had a purpose and, in turn, gave others a purpose as well. I wanted to be a teacher—a teacher who looked at each student with promise and potential, a teacher who defied all odds to become the confident woman that many know today as Dr. Buss.

My school experience had started at a small, local Catholic school. In second grade, it became obvious that I was not learning the material in the areas of reading, writing, or math, like my peers. I remember being in the classroom completely confused about words that were being presented on the board or in front of me while looking at our books. I remember a conversation I had with myself, saying: *How are my friends knowing what to say when the teachers call on them to read? How are they making sense of the letters to form these things called "words?"* I remember thinking as well: *Why can't I read them? Why does this not make sense to me? Try harder. Look harder.* But, when the teacher called on me, the answers always came back as silence. At this point in school, I would find other things to do in class—making up my own stories, looking at the pictures in the book, turning each page, and investigating the pictures to create my own characters. This entertained me and was the only way I knew how to attack the reading.

I recall loving and paying such close attention when the teacher would read to us. I loved when her voice would change, and she acted like each of the characters in the book. I would look straight at her while she read, never following along in my book. I remember getting in trouble for this action, but at those moments I wanted to know the real story. I wanted to hear the words I was unable to read. In these moments, I felt a part of the class and not lost and wished that we did reading this way every day.

I also remember working one-on-one with the teacher during guided reading group. I vividly remember that my words were different from the groups' words. The teacher and I were working on two- or three-letter words. When the teacher was working with the other groups, I would be able to hear them, and I knew at that point that I was different because my activities included basic and small words, while the other groups were reading fast, learning bigger words, and spelling them. In my group, I hesitated to make each sound and never really read any of the books or pages by myself. I also couldn't fake my story. My teacher would not let me just tell a story based on the pictures. The teacher constantly reminded me to look at the words listed at the bottom of the page, not to simply use visual details.

At this young age, it was difficult to manage the frustrations of not being able to do what seemed so easy for everyone else. I felt helpless. I would lash out by yelling and ripping my assignments to shreds. I was overwhelmed. I was frustrated. I wanted to learn it differently. I wanted more one-on-one instruction, so I asked to have materials read aloud to me. And I asked for words to be spelled to me. My teachers, in a class of thirty, became increasingly annoyed with my constant asking for help when they had so many other students who learned without any additional supports. I continued to fall behind, and this caused my teachers to become concerned about how I would comprehend the material. Eventually, my parents were asked to come in to speak with my teacher, who had no solutions for helping me make more progress within the classroom. Instead, my teacher informed my parents that I would have to seek an education elsewhere.

I was diagnosed with a learning disability within the areas of reading, writing, and mathematics, and the Catholic school I attended didn't have the resources or services to support my learning needs. I was asked to leave and attend the local public school where they had support services for students with specific learning disabilities. At the time, I really didn't understand the impact of those words until I realized one thing: I was unwanted by the school. I didn't belong. Rejection. Rejection is hard enough to encounter as an adult; as a child, it's even harder to bear.

From then on, I decided to take school day by day. I was exposed to a variety of different teaching styles and strategies, including small group instruction, pre-teaching, books on tape, readers for tests and quizzes, dictation of written work, extended time, and copies of guided notes. I would use most of these strategies throughout my educational journey. At the time, I didn't realize how effective these were for my learning. The strategies were truly gifts that afforded me academic success, one step at time.

One particular example comes to mind when I was learning how to spell in fourth grade. I remember one of my teachers saying, "Jenny, I am not going to spell this word out for you. You need to use the dictionary and look it up yourself." Well, to any other child, that would seem like an obvious solution, but I did not learn like the other children. To me, the dictionary was the complete opposite of a tool. It felt like the words got lost in the woods, and I had to try to help them out without a flashlight or a map. Even though I was not a skilled word scout, I did master the ability to memorize the physical features of the dictionary. I can vividly recall how that 1,000-page, red book felt and how it smelled when I ruffled through the pages. Anything beyond explaining the physical appearance of the book involved serious effort and time. When given a word to find, I was only able to identify the first letter of the word I was trying to spell. The rest was like a foreign concept to me. The extensiveness of the English vernacular is remarkable— the number of words listed within the "D" section alone was close to 10,000. My identification of only the first letter in the word would not be enough to identify the rest of the spelling. As a result, I was forced to come up with alternative ways to learn how to spell and write out words. I began to select words that I knew how to spell already or to locate the smaller words that

were within a bigger word. Most of these tricks needed to be developed because I was never able to learn phonics. So instead, I did what I was learning to do—the next best thing—adapt.

Since every teacher had different teaching styles and organizations in their classrooms, I would have to adapt to what type of teacher they were. First, which was most important to me, I had to determine their willingness to adjust to different styles of teaching: Would they offer a copy of the notes? Would they provide visuals? Would they repeat directions? Would they offer step-by-step directions? I felt, with each teacher, I had to adapt to their ways of teaching and ask for these strategies when they were not provided. This caused me to find my voice. My attention to these details supported my success as I continued my educational journey.

By the time junior high rolled around, I began to finally accept my unique learning situation and celebrated my own successes, however small they may have been. I began to set certain goals for myself that were realistic and attainable for my specific academic abilities. While many kids expected A's on their assignments, I strove for C's. I acknowledged what I excelled at and continued to work on the areas I struggled with. Some of these accomplishments were harder to congratulate myself on when my struggles seemed to overshadow them. For example, I can recall the year I took the ACT. As a high school student at the time, I was eligible to take the exam. While some

> **"**
>
> I remember thinking: *How can someone talk about something that they're considered an expert on when they're not practicing it in their own setting?* ... As I walked out of class that day, I was determined to challenge her beliefs and show her what I was capable of.
>
> **"**

of my classmates celebrated their scores, I was left stunned and utterly embarrassed as I found out I received the same score as an astronaut monkey: thirteen. I was transported back to the emotions and pain I felt after being moved to another school because I was "unteachable" as a small child. I always tried to move past defining myself as unwanted, but now I was also stuck seeing myself as a number—a number that forced my counselors to encourage me to work at the mall instead of pursuing a career in education; a number that not only discouraged me, but, remarkably, pushed me to further define myself instead of letting outside factors define me. I realized that I needed to take another path in order to continue my education.

This new path included my attending a junior college instead of immediately throwing myself into a four-year university. As I started at the junior college, I had to take some remedial classes even before the 100-level courses. Whereas some students would have been offended by the suggestion of taking these classes, I took it as an opportunity to truly learn and prepare for the challenging classes ahead. I accomplished this one assignment at a time,

one class at a time, and one success at a time. I also reminded myself that I needed to set the same type of realistic goals for myself that I had previously set in high school. As I moved through my classes, I saw progress. I saw and began to understand what it was like to be a learner, actually learning the material. For the first time, I read my own chapter book that was required in the English class. I wrote my first essay using dictation. I re-read material and was able to write summaries about what I read, and I was using larger vocabulary in my conversations and writing. I was able to sit in an entire class and not be overwhelmed or frustrated. I actually participated in class verbally and with written work. And I was able to engage in small group instruction. I was learning and keeping up with my peers.

While at Joliet Junior College, I decided that I wanted to be a teacher. I wanted to be there for the learners who have similar academic struggles and teach them the strategies, show them understanding, and inspire them. For this reason, I went on to attend Illinois State University to major in special education. The classes were so informative, as if they were about my own educational journey. I thoroughly enjoyed learning about why I learn the way I do and other ways to incorporate inclusive practices into the classroom. I became excited, obsessed even, to learn about how teachers can allow all students to be an integral part of classroom learning. Learning about these concepts and strategies reminded me of the hours I would spend on homework. But when I looked back on those many moments, I realized that applying these practices and strategies actually paid off in a positive way in my life. And I realized, too, that I had something that some of the professors couldn't explain from their research. I had something that couldn't be taught. I lived it, and I could connect with the learners more than my peers could. For the first time in my educational career, I had an advantage. I was getting As in my classes and finally being recognized for my hard work.

After I graduated with my bachelor's degree, I worked for five years as an Inclusion Specialist in junior high in the K-12 school system. I then transferred to a high school multi-needs position where I stayed for ten years, creating and developing programs and curriculum in the areas of reading and mathematics. While at the high school, I finished my master's in educational leadership, thinking that one day I might want to run a school. As life proceeded, I had five children, became part-time at the high school, and taught as an adjunct faculty member at a local college where I was teaching future teachers in a class called "The Exceptional Learner." While I thoroughly enjoyed teaching at the high school and never really saw myself teaching in higher education, I instantly fell in love with teaching future teachers. I loved the class. I loved the students. I loved the thought of impacting the future of many students to come. As life happened, another opportunity presented itself: I was asked to work full-time at Lewis University, and so I left my high school position.

After taking the position at Lewis University, and to remain as a full-time employee, I was informed that I would need to get a Ph.D. At this time, I also had five children ranging from five months to seven years. *How was I to work full time, be a wife, and raise five children, and embark on the highest degree you can earn in a subject area?* Well, that journey again began—now at the University of Illinois Chicago—with one class at a time. I never really considered how long it would take me to complete the entire degree. Instead, I thought about how much I could take away from each of the courses. I believe this mindset helped me to be grounded and realistic. I vividly remember people stopping to ask me what I was always working on as I took advantage of the small windows of time presented between my children's plethora of activities.

During these hectic moments, I had time to reflect upon my own values. I strongly believe that there is a plan for each and every one of us. God has laid out this plan from the very beginning, fully aware of what we can do, will do, and how we will do it. I continued to put my trust and faith in God all throughout this journey. I have always taken the path less traveled, not to be an awe-inspiring trailblazer, but because this is the path that works for me, the same plan that God always knew was right for me.

For the five years during my doctoral program, my day would begin with studying from 4:30 a.m. to about 6:30 a.m. I would go for a run, wake up the kids, and get them ready for their day. The oldest four of my five would go to school all day, five days a week, while my youngest would go for only half days. I would take advantage of every free moment by sneaking in some extra study time while naps were going on or the kids were at their activities. I would work full days on Tuesday and Thursdays, even teaching in the evening. On Wednesdays, I would work all day and take my doctoral classes in the evening. After class, I would stay in Chicago until the library closed, and then I would head home. Saturdays and Sundays would be days of heading back to the city, meeting with my tutors, and sometimes even meeting my instructors to finish studying or working on my projects.

I had many positive experiences in my graduate courses, especially the teachers that went above and beyond teaching me—pre-teaching me material, reviewing concepts in different ways, providing copies of notes or additional problems to do so I would understand the material. I even had professors who would meet me on Saturdays and Sundays to review drafts of chapters and writing samples. They would also provide me with additional material to read to grasp certain concepts further. Most importantly, they treated me with respect and were as enthusiastic to teach me as I was to learn. They looked at me more as a person who was eager to learn more about the field, not as a disabled person. I experienced a truly open-door policy, a policy that not only benefitted me greatly but made me realize what education was supposed to be.

But there were instances when I was questioned because of my accommodations. I recall a Special Education professor asking me, "What do you mean you need extra time on the test, a copy of the notes, and extra office hour time?" She taught *about* students with disabilities, but she had never actually *had* a student at this level who exemplified the characteristics about which she taught. She was utterly taken back about how I, with a learning disability, was able to be in a doctoral program. This was disheartening. I remember thinking: *How can someone talk about something that they're considered an expert on when they're not practicing it in their own setting?* To her question, I responded, "I am that kid you are going to accommodate in your class. I am that kid you teach us about. Now it's your turn to practice what you preach." As I walked out of class that day, I was determined to challenge her beliefs and show her what I was capable of. My determination paid off, as I received the highest grade in the class for that semester. Along with my outstanding grade, I also ended up receiving a personal apology from my professor. These doubts from my professor inspired me to look deeper into higher education faculty members' perceptions of disabilities. These concerns drove me to find ways to prove them wrong within my own dissertation. These doubts allowed me to become the teacher I always dreamed I could be.

On the day I defended my dissertation, my emotions were high, and my level of anxiety was nearly out of control. I gave the children a kiss as they got on the bus, and said, "Today is the day mommy will become Dr. Buss." Later, as I walked into the room to defend my dissertation, I thanked God again for this amazing journey and the opportunity to learn and to further my education. After almost two hours of defending my dissertation, through the many questions from the committee and the audience, I walked out of the room for them to deliberate. I hugged my husband and fell into his arms, exhausted. I recall saying over and over again, "I gave it everything. I did the best I could. Please, let this be done." The door opened, and my committee chair looked right at me and said, "Congratulations, Dr. Buss." My heart swelled up into my throat, and, for the first time in a very long time, I had nothing to say. I began to cry. Hugs were exchanged and applause could be heard while I entered the room again to sign the papers. After our short celebration inside, my husband and I went to Starbucks to get some food and to reward myself with my favorite Starbucks order. I ordered my usual, and when the barista asked me for a name, I looked right at him with the biggest smile on my face as I responded, "Dr. Buss!"

So, what did I actually end up doing? Well, I have been teaching for twenty-five years in special education. Nearly half of my career was spent in the K-12 system, and the last fifteen years in higher education teaching future teachers. I earned my bachelor's degree from Illinois State University in special education and my master's in educational leadership from Aurora University. I earned my Ph.D. from the University of Illinois Chicago in special education focusing on the success of students with learning disabilities in higher education and program design for all students in inclusive settings.

The name *Dr. Buss* means so much more to me than just knowing a lot about special education. It means that anything is possible if we follow the path God has planned for us, no matter the difficulty. Coming from someone who went from L.D. to Ph.D., the challenge is sometimes the opportunity. You just have to recognize it.

Bump, Wright, Calder, Me

by Leslie Ansteth Colonna, M.F.A.

Assistant Professor, Department of Art and Design

Early in life, I decided I wanted to be an artist of some sort.

In an old family photo album, still on a bookshelf somewhere in my parents' house, is an 8 x 10 glossy black and white photograph. It is of my grandfather, Bump, standing with the architect Frank Lloyd Wright. I first saw the photograph when I was about seven. For some reason, I remember it. You can see both men's whole bodies. My grandfather is dressed in a suit, and he's wearing a hat and little round glasses. I think Wright is also wearing a hat. It's not a posed photograph. It looks like they might be outside on a building site. The two men are looking at each other and talking. I suspect my father might have taken the photograph to document this somewhat special moment. My grandfather was a landscape architect. There wasn't much of a story to go with the photograph. As I remember, my parents told me that Bump had worked for Wright on one of his spectacular new buildings, the Price Tower, which was to be the corporate headquarters of an oil pipeline company near my grandfather's business in Tulsa, Oklahoma. The building had originally been designed for New York City but was never built there. Wright even nicknamed it "The Tree that Escaped the Crowded Forest" meaning the forest of Manhattan skyscrapers. The story I was told was Wright wanted a large tree installed on the nineteenth-floor penthouse of his tiny, new skyscraper, that the job was difficult because the elevators in the building were tiny, that much care had to be taken not to damage the interior of the building, and that Wright had chosen my grandfather to do the project. Hearing the story as a kid, I only understood that my grandfather was doing something important. But maybe it also made me think about who I was in relation to my family history. I think the photograph showed me a snapshot of where I came from.

In the 1920s, some forty years before this moment, my grandfather had started his landscape design business. By the time I was around, and saw that photograph, my parents had taken over the business and were continuing the same specialized design and installation landscape work my grandfather had done. The company still used many of the methods Bump started all those years earlier. What was so formative for me was the environment. Our house was next to the business, which consisted of a large tree nursery and several outbuildings. Over the years, the nursery had grown into a beautiful, wooded acreage, and I spent much of my time at the business, after school and on weekends. Although I didn't appreciate it then, I think back on how magical it was there. The office was in a large warehouse, and it was full, I mean full, of a conglomeration of machines, drafting tables, huge flat drawer files full of architectural blueprints, photographs of building sites, archaic drawing tools, rubber stamps of trees, typewriters, ledgers, pruning shears, creaky office chairs, stained coffee cups, horticultural and architectural design magazines, and more, and usually a dog. The outbuildings also had a quarter century of accumulation in them. There were shovel parts, saws, wheelbarrows, stacks and stacks of burlap bags and garden hoses, sprinkler parts, more machines, large drums full of grass seed, gas cans, trucks, strange old tools, and machines, left over from my grandfather, some of them still in use and some frozen from age and rust. One was so beautiful it is still in my parents' yard looking like a Julio Gonzales sculpture, an elegant jumble of metal rods and cylinders, evocative of a figure, or a plant, standing in the middle of the grass just beyond the patio. Something was always being built, designed, sketched, dug up, planted, irrigated, innovated, broken, welded, fixed, saved, redesigned, repurposed, tied, cut, clamped, lifted, salvaged, invented, found, lost, stolen, found again, torn down, or rebuilt. Looking back, the "building" as we called it, would have been the greatest art studio possible, and in my childhood, I kind of used it as such, watching and learning from my father, as I messed around with whatever tools and materials I could. I grew up getting more and more comfortable using my hands and the tools that were available to me. This was the environment where my interests in art took hold. In school, then, science and art were the most enjoyable classes to me. They were places where I could look at things, use tools, experiment, and design and invent new things with my hands.

I went to college far away from home to study ceramics and art history at Mills College in California. I then transferred to Skidmore College in upstate New York, drawn to the beauty in the old cities, bridges, and landscapes of New England, and where I found a school that better suited me. I took a semester off from college, and my family got together and built an adobe house from scratch, in New Mexico. It was a scheme of my parents as a vacation home, and designed by my brother, a young architect. I graduated college and spent several years back home teaching and managing the ceramics department at Philbrook Art Center. I got my MFA in sculpture from

Cranbrook Art Academy. I married my wonderful and brilliant Dominic, and we had the two most beautiful children in the world, and we lived in New Haven, Connecticut. Family life! I showed and taught here and there. I went back to school again and received my teaching certification in Art. I taught in arts magnet middle and secondary schools in New Haven and gained valuable pedagogical experience that I still use today, in assessment, interdisciplinary learning, and critical thinking. Soon, Dom was offered a position at Lewis University, and we moved to Illinois. Lewis offered me a position as an adjunct instructor. Now, as a full-time assistant professor, I am lucky to be able to help students learn how to make art, how to think about it critically, historically, and ethically, and how to apply their art to their professional career or higher academic studies.

Along my way toward arriving where I am now, I have found kindred spirits in the art world whose work reminded me of all the ways of doing things that I learned as a child, from my family and the environment I grew up in. They are my mentors, alive or dead, who hold the same values that I developed from my childhood through graduate school. I regularly return to them for inspiration in making and teaching art. One is Alexander Calder. Maybe more than anything, perhaps it was Calder's huge famous art studio that he renovated from a barn in rural Connecticut that I first felt an affinity to. It had the same creative energy that was in the "building" at my grandfather's nursery. In historical photos and videos, Calder's studio was dynamic and alive, a huge mess if you didn't know better. I imagined a little of Calder was in me, my father, and my grandfather. He was famous for working across mediums and for his innovations. He was loved for his delightful forms, which ranged from toys to monumental sculptures. To explain the essence of his work, he told of a transcendent moment in his life as he observed, simultaneously, the sun setting in the west and the moon rising in the east. He said, "...the underlying sense of form in my work has been the system of the Universe, or part thereof" (Calder 8-9). His family history of artists and his training as an engineer made him an inventor as much as an artist. Look at a Calder and you see a celebration of making, what he was thinking, how he solved a problem. His creations were as much exercises in physics as they were aesthetic expressions. He is credited for inventing the mobile as an artform, the largest of which hangs in the National Gallery of Art in Washington, D.C. His creativity seemed to be born out of his observation of the forces in nature, his sense of awe, and his ability to imagine these ideas in new materials, all things that I find deeply moving. To me, Calder's art is a celebration of the physical world and a beautiful expression of the creative human spirit.

Although I am no Alexander Calder, learning about his ideas and methods encouraged me to pursue my love of making things. I work in all mediums, but my interest in clay is an example of this aspiration. I began studying ceramics seriously in high school. At first, clay seemed so basic, but every step in my studies sparked my curiosity and taught me new things. Among my adventures, I built my own kiln in New Mexico, learned the chemistry of glazes and the physics of reduction and oxidation, mined my own clay from riverbeds and hills, and more than once found myself asking ranchers for their livestock manure to fuel my kiln. Ceramics also taught me about cultures and history. Art made from clay can be anything—from the form of a beautiful, functional pot to an abstract sculpture. I studied everything from Japanese tea ceremony pottery to sculpture from the California Funk movement. I loved it all and continue to this day to learn and be inspired to create new things.

As a teacher, Calder is one of a myriad of artists I use to teach students about the intrinsic value of art for its own sake, the joy one can get from looking at art or making art, and the applied value of art when it is used in the service of another area of study. I am happy that current educational research seems to have caused a sustained surge in support for art, design, and visual literacy in schools and universities. Much has been said recently about the value of studying art for its own sake and for use in other areas. For example, Harvard Medical School and numerous other universities now offer courses in studying visual arts to expand medical students' abilities to observe, describe, analyze, and develop hypotheses through teamwork. Similar programs, like one at The National Gallery of Art, and another called Visual Thinking Strategies, are being promoted in primary and secondary level schools. At Stanford University, David Kelley has built a whole school around design thinking and creative problem solving for application in other professions.

Bump, Wright, Calder, and me. That is my little history. When I meet my students, I wonder about their personal stories that have led them into my classroom. I wonder how they are already creative, either in art or another discipline. Born out of my own love, wonder, and appreciation for art and the creative human spirit, I hope to give my students experiences to spark their curiosity and to develop their visual acuity, discernment, and their own unique creative skills—skills they can apply to both their personal and professional life, and use for their whole life.

Works Cited

Calder, Alexander. "What Abstract Art Means to Me." *Museum of Modern Art Bulletin 18*, no.3, 1951, 8-9. www.calder.org/bibliography/the-museum-of-modern-art-bulletin-1951/.

▲ **ARTWORK BY LESLIE ANSTETH COLONNA.** *Clockwise from top left:* Portrait of Georgia O'Keeffe. Glazed earthenware and oil paint. *Figure Study after Jean-Baptiste Carpeaux. Earthenware. Figure for Arrowmont.* Glazed stoneware. *Portrait of Elizabeth Catlett.* Glazed earthenware and oil paint. *Portrait of Marcel Duchamp.* Earthenware. *Portrait of Millicent Rogers.* Glazed earthenware and oil paint. *Figure for Diane's Garden.* Glazed stoneware. *The Aesop Series: Telling the Fox Fables.* Glazed earthenware.

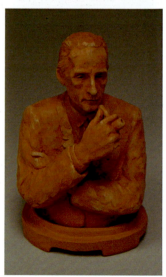

School as a Site of Struggle, Resistance, and Hope

by Erica R. Dávila, Ph.D.

Professor, Department of Education
Program Director of Educational Leadership

My life story and my educational experiences and inquiries are one and the same. My experiences in school shaped so much of who I am. When I started formal schooling in Chicago in the early 1980s, I had no idea that I was entering a school system that had been and would be analyzed, researched, and discussed all around the nation: the Chicago Public Schools (CPS). In this school system, I was teased about how I spoke. At around age nine, when my classmates and I transitioned from bilingual education, I recall a lot of name-calling, some about language but mostly about our Latinx ethnicities. "Puddle jumper," "wetback," "beaner," "spic," "me no speak English" were all terms and phrases I recall, and not just from students. Teachers, "joking" around, also used some of these terms. I was trying to navigate my bilingual tongue in the social world of the schoolhouse where English was recognized as the holy grail, and any signs of other languages and dialects were not the same as a pure, monolingual English.

During the fall of my sixth grade, then Secretary of Education, William Bennet, publicly called CPS the worst schools in our nation; I do not recall him saying this in 1987 (I was eleven years old), but instead, about a decade later, when I was studying to be a teacher. I studied elementary education and sociology, and these two disciplines gave me the language, the research, and the validation that I needed, and still need, to understand the ways schools work as sites of struggle, resistance, and hope. Understanding this context was important to me because, like most kids at this age, I internalized my experiences and blamed myself when I was teased and bullied.

Educational scholars have problematized school as a place that strips many children of their own selves. Some of the research distinguishes between education versus schooling, arguing that we can educate without being "schooled." Schooling is the process of following rules and regulations, while education is a process of genuine curiosity and learning. Schools are both the place where some flourish and others are socialized to dim their light, or worse, to feel disposable. As someone who has spent her life in schools, I want to think about the layers of struggle, resistance, and hope that these institutions—and more importantly, the people inside of them—can offer us.

School as a Site of Struggle

The first thing the school system did was label me as "other." My five-year-old self entered as an emerging bilingual speaker—English and Spanish—with strong, early literacy skills and even stronger math skills, learning my multiplication tables before kindergarten, thanks to my father, one of my first teachers. But the school system only focused on how much English I knew. I was placed in a transitional bilingual program, and I was thrilled. All my classmates and teachers looked and sounded just like me. My mom was very present in the classroom, and we celebrated all the same holidays, with the same delicious foods, as I did at home. It felt like an extension of home with a bunch of friends! As I progressed in my English speaking and writing abilities, I was mainstreamed in the fourth grade to an all-English classroom. It was traumatic. In my first four years (kindergarten through third grade), since I was so focused on my English, I never realized how much of my Spanish the school was taking from me.

My transition to fourth grade was socially and emotionally very hard; I felt like I did not belong because most of my peers did not look or sound like me. Little did my nine-year-old self understand that part of this trauma was the stripping of my native tongue, a vital part of me. At the time, it was very clear that the bilingual kids were seen and treated as "other." I had a hard time socially and wanted to fit it in and not be "othered." As I got older, I started to really feel the weight of the loss of my Spanish. I recall talking less and less Spanish at home and panicking when I met, for the first time, relatives from Puerto Rico who spoke only Spanish. I later realized that I was experiencing a form of linguistic discrimination—the attempted extinguishing of my home language—with the ultimate goal of learning English at the expense of my bilingualism.

About a decade later, school policies came for my language again. I was placed in Spanish I in high school because I could barely write it since Spanish instruction completely stopped before the fourth grade; my Spanish literacy was still at a third-grade level, possibly lower. I did not like Spanish class because it made me realize how the school system took my Spanish from me and stifled my bilingualism. Another struggle I had in Spanish classes was the "othering" of my dialect. The Spanish they were trying to teach me was not my language, was not my Spanish. *My* Spanish was rooted in Puerto Rico with influences from our indigenous ancestors who were Taino, our African ancestors through enslavement and the colonizers from Spain. It was not the Spanish that my instructor and most of academia values, the Spanish that comes directly from Europe. I had a similar experience in a college course with the instructor clearly and publicly telling me (and a friend), "Aqui no se habla ese español," or "Here we do not speak that Spanish." I later learned that she was referring to our Puerto Rican dialect.

Luckily, I had family and mentors that helped me regain my bilingualism, although it is something I have to always practice. I know how detrimental the loss of those early years in my language development were—a deliberate function of school policies. I share this narrative because, as a professor in the field of education, I know how rampant linguistic discrimination in schools is, and I will continue to fight this struggle. We must honor, treasure, and, most importantly, cultivate all the linguistic diversity that enters our schools—not just respecting all mother tongues that come to the schoolhouse, but doing what we can to cultivate them. This includes offering multilingual texts and multilingual resources, such as books, family communications, extracurricular information, and other communications and curriculum unique to each school community.

School as a Site of Resistance

I would like to introduce you to my mother. Mami was born in Cidra, Puerto Rico, and migrated along with her older sister and my grandma right before her entry in the school system in New York City (NYC). She does not talk much about school in NYC, but what she does share is awful, which explains why there is not much joy in her retelling her story of schooling. One specific story she did share with me connects to my own above: Mami was bilingual as well, but instead of slowly stripping her Spanish from her as they did to me in Chicago in the 1980s, her experience in NYC in the 1960s was much more traumatic, with nuns smacking her and my aunt for speaking Spanish in the school yard. She resisted and is beautifully fluent, speaking both English and Spanish. And in spite of the schools' attempts to erase her language (and my own), she never stopped hablando en español, and she made sure my brother and I ultimately kept our bilingualism.

School as a Site of Hope

There has to be something you are struggling *for*. For me, fueled by my current work as an educational leader in higher education, that something is hope. While I was a classroom teacher in Urbana, Illinois, where I accepted a fifth-grade teaching position after graduating college, I decided to enroll in graduate school. While working on my Master of Education degree, my advisor recruited me for the doctoral program. I was not sure about this big decision, though I am glad I made that decision because my graduate program helped shape my vocation and made my life's calling much clearer. This calling was not just about teaching, but consistently engaging my sociological imagination when it comes to educational inequities. Sociological imagination is a fancy way of saying that we think about and address the social influences that guide our decisions and the decisions of others. While in my undergraduate sociology program, I studied the history of social injustices in our nation; my graduate program, however, is where my analysis of the role of schooling in these social injustices crystallized. I began to really understand all those early school experiences of my own, my family, and my community.

My entrance into the academy as a professor clarified policies and practices that were designed for children like me to fail: poor children, children of color, children in disinvested urban school districts, children who enter school as emerging English learners, children whose parents have limited formal schooling. Entire bodies of research on each of these categories demonstrate the ways in which school is not a place for them. With every class I taught, every paper I published, and every student I mentored, I became more emboldened to share my story of deficit, a story that some may see as shameful. I

have no shame. Instead, I am proud of my story and the ways in which the struggle and resistance inform my hope and my actions toward educational equity, especially for the categories of children I listed above. The field of education has a lot of work to do to become just and to serve all children. The reality is that many children in the system will experience school as nothing more than a site of struggle, but hopefully, they too will resist.

I have faith that schools can be a site of hope, that we can transform the ways in which children experience school— one teacher, one assignment, one school at a time. We all have the power to shift deficit narratives and to refresh or rebuild hope within schools—by questioning student placements, language learning approaches, school curriculum, disciplinary policies, assessment procedures, parent and community involvement, teacher training, and principal preparation. These are just a few of the areas that research has shown to be unjust and/or outdated, and that I question in my work and with my students— students who are teachers, community leaders, and principals. I support their work with their students and communities, and I build structures that nurture our students in my college classrooms, in my scholarship, and in community work.

I urge you to find *your* sphere of influence, where you can create school as a site of hope. *We all have a sphere of influence. We just need to find it.*

How I Found Myself

by Bryan Durkin, M.B.A.

Class of '82 and '94
Member of the Lewis University Board of Trustees

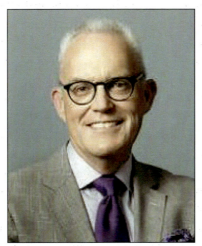

It is hard to believe as I write this story about my life's journey that it was forty-three years ago that I found myself as a seventeen-year-old young man starting college at Lewis University. At this point in my life, I lacked confidence in myself as I was not an academic achiever in high school, nor was I athletic or part of the "cool" group. However, I knew that I had an inherent compassion for helping people—which was part of my family culture—and musical talent. As an adolescent, my parents were amazingly supportive and patient, investing their time and money into my musical training. While many thought that I aspired to be a professional musician, this was not the case. I remember feeling lost inside of myself, as I did not have the desire to pursue this path. But I also felt that there were no other options for my future.

With the guidance of my music instructors, I applied to the School of Music at the University of Illinois Urbana-Champaign and was accepted into their program. However, when it came time to commit, I shocked my parents by telling them I would not pursue this opportunity. I did not have the passion for a music career and felt that I would ultimately fail to complete the program. My parents were naturally surprised and disappointed, but they patiently supported my decision. They also made it very clear that not attending college was not an option for me and that I would attend college, just as my three older siblings had.

My father sat me down to relate that he had arranged a meeting with a Christian Brother from Lewis University, where my older brother and sister had both attended. After meeting with me, Lewis University decided to accept me on academic probation due to my lackluster high school grades. In hindsight, I attribute my poor academic high school record to lack of confidence in myself, floundering with minimal guidance in a large high school. I attribute my personal and professional happiness and success to my experiences at this university. Lewis believed in this directionless, young man, accepted me into their community, and helped to mold and guide me into the man that I am today.

I recall vividly my first day of orientation as an incoming freshman when this beautiful, young woman named Mary Connelly arrived late to the orientation and was assigned to my group. I was instantly awe-struck by this person and immediately knew that I was going to marry her someday. Whenever I tell this story, people react to me with much skepticism, but it is the truth! Mary had also been accepted to the University of Illinois but chose Lewis because the size of the Lewis campus was more conducive to her comfort zone, and Lewis was also offering her more in scholarship funding. I am convinced that divine intervention was involved in bringing us both together at Lewis.

Once the first week of school started, I reached out to Mary, who was majoring in Business Administration. She inquired about my major, which was Public Administration. She shared with me that because of her profound hearing impairment, she would need the support of a notetaker in her classes to capture the content of each lecture. She wondered if I would be willing to switch majors to support her in this regard. Given my mad crush on her, I was happy to switch majors, and that is where our romance and life's journey began. We have been together for forty-three years and married for thirty-seven.

It was very intimidating for me to commit to being Mary's primary notetaker for the next four years as I knew she was a strong student, dependent on an academic scholarship, and already had a semester of CLEP credits to accelerate her college record. Yet, she was willing to become fully reliant on me to capture our lectures for the forthcoming four years. I recognized that I was barely a C student in high school and did not remotely have any of the scholastic ambition or drive that she possessed. Upon disclosing all this to Mary, she responded that I was severely underestimating myself and saw intelligence and capabilities in me that I couldn't see for myself. Thanks to her efforts in teaching me excellent study habits and helping me with my focus challenges, I managed to develop an amazing ability to transcribe copious lecture notes. These notes helped us both, and we ultimately graduated from the College of Business with High Honors.

Lewis' faculty and community helped me to believe in myself; they pushed me to develop the confidence in my ability to contribute, learn, thrive, and succeed. I could list many names of faculty and staff members who took personal interest in helping me as a student. These mentors sought to fortify my business skills and grant me valuable exposure through my work experiences with the College of Business or with the university's business office. Every step of the way, there were people who impacted me in such a profound way, which encouraged me to develop a deep passion for learning. This passion ultimately positioned me to help many students along the way to thrive through my experiences as a tutor and teaching assistant for the College of Business. I felt extremely blessed to have been given these incredible opportunities, which ultimately led me to pursue my MBA at Lewis. I would also become an adjunct faculty member in the College of Business, teaching courses in business at both the undergraduate and graduate level. Keep in mind, all these achievements evolved from a seventeen-year-old directionless teenager who lacked confidence or belief in himself. His high school counselor had advised him to give up on the prospect of attending college as, "You are not college material." Thank God my parents believed otherwise, as did my future wife, and the many wonderful people at Lewis who were willing to take a chance on me and help me to prove otherwise.

My undergraduate graduation from Lewis was a daunting experience for me as I was now a man, completely responsible for myself and needing to find a full-time career. Every graduating senior experiences this feeling of uncertainty about graduation, i.e., *How do I begin my career search? What do I want to do with my life? Where will I end up?* These are all natural questions for seniors to ask themselves. I entered the job market in 1982 when unemployment was at one of its highest levels in history. Luckily for me, all throughout college, I had maintained a part-time job at Mercy Hospital, located in the inner city of Chicago. It brought me great joy to assist patients with their recoveries and to comfort those with terminal illnesses. There was one patient

whom I cared for, a Sister of Mercy who took great interest in my career search. She was a highly respected administrator and well known throughout the city of Chicago. She circulated my résumé to numerous business contacts, hoping to help me network.

This Sister of Mercy, Sister Mary Huberta, RSM, was my role model and inspiration for what it was like to be a great leader. She was also a woman of immense compassion for helping others. Through her efforts, I began getting calls for job interviews. One company in particular, the Chicago Board of Trade (now called the CME Group), offered me a full-time job as an investigator in their regulatory division. This was a very intimidating opportunity as I knew nothing of the financial futures markets. But I did know that I possessed deep perseverance and a commitment to learning, so I would be able to develop the knowledge and skills to become successful in my new role. This was the beginning of an amazing and blessed thirty-eight-year career, which spanned many exciting roles and responsibilities—from Staff Investigator to Chief of Market Regulation, Chief Operating Officer, Chief Commercial Officer and, ultimately, to President of the CME Group. In each of these roles, I was both fortunate and blessed to have opportunities to challenge myself by learning the technical and operational inner workings of the highly complex financial futures and options markets (something I never imagined myself capable of doing), taking on highly complex responsibilities by pursuing opportunities to do so, being dedicated and focused on delivering results, developing strong relationships with knowledge experts, each of whom took interest in me to mentor and help cultivate my technical and leadership skills, and always exhibiting patience, diplomacy, and a genuine passion for each role that I performed. From the beginning of my college days, Lewis' mission of Signum Fidei—Sign of Faith—became deeply embedded in my values and into my soul. I have relied on this foundation to ground and guide me in my professional and personal life.

After receiving our undergraduate degrees, Mary and I married at the age of twenty-three years old, began our career journeys, started a family, and achieved our MBAs from Lewis while working full time and raising three children. We both taught courses at Lewis, had one more biological child, adopted two children from China, led successful careers, and are now happily retired as the parents of six children and three grandchildren. Now, reflecting on these days, it's hard to believe all that we were able to juggle at such a young age. I owe it all to my wife Mary. The number one foundation of my life's happiness and both personal and professional success begins and ends with her. If you note one theme throughout this paper, it's about learning to believe in yourself and having people in your life that believe in you. Mary has always been that one constant in my life, and anyone who has met her would attest that she has this effervescent, positive attitude

about life. Her outlook on life is simple: "You can conquer anything in life as long as you believe in yourself and put your mind to facing challenges and opportunities with a positive attitude."

People constantly are intrigued by the size of our family. Mary and I always had the desire to have a large family, and oddly to this day, people continue to ask us why we didn't stop having children after having four biological children. The answer for us was simple: Very early into our marriage, prior to having our four daughters, we lost our first child. We tried to conceive afterwards for a couple of years and were experiencing great difficulties doing so and suffered more miscarriages along the way. We decided at that time to focus on adoption, and both of us were drawn to China for no specific reason other than we knew there were many orphans there without a home or family. However, as we began to seriously consider this path, Mary became pregnant through our fertility efforts, and over the ensuing eight years we were blessed with four biological children. Years later, it bothered both of us that we never followed through with our adoption efforts. Hence, well into our late forties, we adopted our first son at the age of six and a half, and two-and-a-half years later, our second son at the age of nine. Both boys, now in their twenties and college students themselves, were abandoned orphans, living in Chinese orphanages with little hope for adoption because they both had serious medical conditions that needed to be addressed. God found a way to bring us all together, and our two boys completed our beautiful family. It is so hard to believe that forty-five years have flown by so quickly. It seems like yesterday that we were walking Lewis' campus grounds as teenage students!

The strongest value that I have learned from my experiences at Lewis is to lead by example: Treat everyone with kindness, respect, and compassion, and bear in mind that there is always someone out there far less fortunate who needs our compassion and support. Mary and I adopted these values and have made it our goal to lead our lives accordingly. It has been our vocation to find ways to share our many blessings with others in a variety of ways—whether it be through sharing our knowledge in teaching courses for our future leaders or continuing to support Lewis University and its students by establishing an endowed scholarship for those who need financial assistance. Additionally, we have chosen to support several charitable and philanthropic efforts to help the underserved, underprivileged, and those in need.

I chose to share these intimate details of my life journey to hopefully encourage future students who are finding their way in life to embrace all that they can about Lewis University, its community, and its mission. I thrived in the smaller university community environment and availed myself to engaging with people in the Lewis community at every step along that journey. Through Lewis' work-study program, as a freshman, I immediately applied for a job in the business office where I was hired to process accounts receivable transactions for the university. Daily, I was interacting with students who were paying their tuition bills, and I met many students through that experience. My favorite work-study experience was serving as a teaching assistant in the College of Business during my sophomore through senior years. I worked for several professors, assisting them with organizing schedules, proctoring exams, and assisting with classes. I also was fortunate to work with the then director of the newly formed MBA program, Tom Dooley, and play a role in developing the program during its formative years. Through these engagements, I was able to develop confidence in myself, evolve and define who I was an individual, and take risks and make mistakes along the way. I pushed myself to develop social and professional skills, which have guided me throughout life's challenging course. I feel so strongly about how Lewis was my guiding light and strength that I have made it my commitment throughout these past forty-three years to remain involved in the Lewis Community and help other aspiring students evolve.

The Influence of One Extraordinary Person

by Melissa Eichelberger, Ed.D.

Class of '88 and '00
Assistant Director, Programming
Department of Academic Services

My parents married and had me at a very young age. My dad was seventeen and my mom, sixteen. They were still children themselves. Their marriage lasted only a short time, and they divorced when I was only four years old. Throughout high school, I did the usual, or what I believed to be the usual: I lived with my mom and visited my dad every other weekend. I also got to see my dad on holidays and for summer vacation. I enjoyed the visits with my dad because we were always doing something. We would go to the beach, go fishing, play volleyball or badminton with my grandparents, aunts, uncles, and cousins—playing outdoor games while roasting a pig or grilling carnitas or arrencheras. We would get together for every occasion—birthdays, anniversaries, holidays, cookouts—or simply just because we could. Our family all lived on the same block, so it was easy to get together. My grandparents had bought the whole block, and my relatives all built their homes on that same street, that same block, in Joliet, Illinois. We spent so much time having fun together. We were all so close. So many times, at the end of my weekend visit, I would cry. I did not want to leave. I wanted more time with my dad and his side of the family. We had a family bond like no other family I have ever known.

One of the best parts of my time with my dad was spending time with my grandparents, especially my grandmother, Santos Cavazos, the matriarch of our family. She started a business at a time when few Hispanics, let alone women, were making a name for themselves. She was doing upholstery work out of her home, removing and replacing furniture coverings and padding with new covers and padding she had sewn together, while my grandpa was making mattresses for Joliet Mattress Factory. My grandma's upholstery business continued to grow, so she moved it out of her home and into bigger quarters. In 1979, they found a vacant warehouse at 4 North Michigan, just behind Joliet's Union Station. In addition to doing the upholstery, they began manufacturing mattresses. The companies were called Cavazos Upholstery and Royal Comfort Mattress. By 1983, our family opened Pattern Designers, a couple blocks away, to make the quilted covers and borders for the mattresses and box springs being made at Royal Comfort.

As I was growing up, I watched my grandma work so hard for her children and all our family. She would do anything for any of us. My grandma would work long hours, head home to cook a wonderful meal, then spend time with my grandpa and any of us that headed to their house for or after dinner. Whenever we were together, she would make every occasion special and make each of us feel special. Growing up, Christmas was always so special. Our family would all gather at my grandparents' house on Christmas Eve morning and spend all day and night there. We would start out by making tamales—well, all the women and girls, anyway—which would take hours to prepare and even longer to steam to perfection. While they cooked, we would play music, sing, and dance. My dad might even play the accordion. Later in the evening, after we were all stuffed from the delicious dinner, we would sit or lay around on the floor and watch a home movie with a huge screen and movie projector with reels of film from the previous year that my aunt

and uncle had recorded during all our family gatherings. Just about the time the movie would end, always right around midnight, all my cousins and I would watch through the window, not-so-patiently waiting for Santa's arrival. He would always come walking and ringing a bell from across the field, carrying a sack of presents over his shoulder. My cousins and I would all get something. Even through all my own excitement, I could see the joy on my grandma's face, and it was priceless. Seeing us happy was what her life was about. After opening gifts, I would head back to my mom's house so that I could wake up with her on Christmas morning. Leaving that night was always so hard.

Although Christmas was especially memorable because of my grandma, taking vacations together was also special. When I was younger, we traveled by car or in a Winnebago to so many places—San Francisco, Salt Lake City, Atlantic City, Daytona, Fort Lauderdale, and Orlando— and many more. Each year, when my grandparents went on vacation, my dad and I would go with them. I was always able to take one of my cousins, too, and sometimes other relatives would also come.

Although we did so much together with my grandmother, there were also times when I would just lay in her lap, or we would sit and talk. She would tell me about the "old times"—about when she was a teenager, married to my grandpa for only a year, and how she went to work with him in an upholstery plant in McLean, Texas. Someone had given her a piece of material to cover a chair. She said she had no idea how it came to her mind, but she knew what to do. That moment began her legacy for our family. She told me about leaving Texas and coming to Illinois in 1954 to work for Dr. John Policondriotes, in his fields. Dr. Polley, as we all called him, owned a grocery store and a significant amount of farmland. Prior to 1954, my great grandfather, Santos Zavaleta, had been working these fields during the summer for years. My grandma, grandpa, dad, aunts, and uncles would pick onions, asparagus, and corn all day long in Dr. Polley's fields, and then go home after a long day. When they got home, my grandma would do upholstery work and cook dinner. My dad was only four years old at the time, so he picked what he could, but mostly played. She told me about how they were just about to head back to Texas at the end of the summer when my dad got sick and had to be hospitalized; he needed emergency surgery on his stomach. My dad's health and slow recovery kept them in Illinois for weeks, then months, until eventually they decided to stay in Illinois and make it their home.

Although my grandmother had planned to return to Texas with her family, her plans and dreams had to change. Her family and my dad's health were much more important than getting back to Texas. She knew that as long as she was with her family, she could make a life in Illinois. She knew they could get through anything as long as they were together. They eventually saved up enough money and purchased a house on Stryker

Avenue in Joliet. She told me how the living room was her work area and how she spent so much time piecing together fabric to reupholster furniture. Sometimes, my grandma's stories could go on and on about her work or how they added onto her house and how eventually she bought the entire block of property on Stryker for her kids to build their houses close to her and my grandpa. She also told me how hard it was when they expanded the family business. They did not even get paid for a while, but they had each other, and having each other meant everything. The bonding and family ties they created starting the business together made it successful.

At the age of fifteen, I was fortunate to begin working in our family businesses through my high school's work-study program. Our shops were within walking distance of Joliet Central High School, so I would leave school and head straight to work. I especially loved when I got out of school early or had days off, so I could work even more. Working for the family business gave me the opportunity to spend so much more time with my dad, aunts, uncles, and grandparents. And everyone truly enjoyed their role within the business. My dad was in sales, my Uncle Frank was managing everything, and my grandma and grandpa were doing the upholstery and making mattresses. My stepmom, aunts, and uncles were also doing upholstery, making mattresses and box springs, quilting the mattress covers, or running the office. It was truly a family affair. I was lucky enough to spend time in the office doing accounts payable, accounts receivable, payroll, and general ledger stuff, along with working in the shop learning from my grandma. She taught me how to take apart furniture, how to sew, how to make mattress borders, and so much more.

I truly enjoyed everything I was able to do in our business, but watching and learning from my grandma meant everything. I watched her work so hard for her children and all our family. She would do anything for any of us. She taught me so much, not just about how to sew or how to reupholster furniture, but about life. My grandma came from a small family with little to her name. She did not come from money and life was always tough. After making the decision to move to Illinois, working so hard in the fields for Dr. Polley, and growing her upholstery business, she was able to save enough money to purchase an entire block of property. This extraordinary act allowed her to keep her family close together. With the support of my grandpa, dad, aunts, and uncles, she then started a business during very difficult economic times. This was another way in which she kept our family close together. Knowing that she could persevere through so many challenges and still be there for her family made her my role model. She inspired me. She was my motivation to work hard every single day. She taught me to be a strong and independent woman. She taught me that family should always come first. And I knew I wanted to be like her when I grew up.

A few years passed, and it was time to grow up and head out on my own for college. Although college was never talked about, as no one in my family had gone to college, I knew I wanted to go. A year and a half earlier, my boyfriend had left on a wrestling scholarship to Southern Illinois University, Edwardsville (SIUE). I decided to graduate high school early so that I could follow him. I wanted to become a lawyer. I thought that I could help other families that went through divorces, like mine. It was hard, though. My family did not know anything about college. As a first-generation, Hispanic, female student, I filled out the application, the financial aid paperwork, packed up my stuff, loaded my car, and drove four hours away— all on my own. My parents did not drive me. They did not move me in. They didn't help me decorate my dorm room. Except for my boyfriend, I was all on my own. And coming from a close-knit family, I hated being so far from them. It was hard. I lasted one year at SIUE. I came home after the fall semester of 1984, and my boyfriend also came home. Rather than go to college, he began working in our family business. After I returned home, I moved in with my dad.

I'll never forget that first morning at my dad's house. He came into my room, woke me up, told me that I was not taking a semester off, and to go out to Lewis University to apply there. Back then, nothing was online. I had to physically head to campus, get the paper application, fill it out, and turn it in. I was accepted and began classes that spring. I was taking classes in

Criminal Justice and working part-time in our family business. At the time, I thought that a major in Criminal Justice was the best route to get me to law school. I quickly realized that Criminal Justice was not for me and that I did not want to become a lawyer after all. I knew, however, that I still wanted to help others in some way. After talking with some friends and my advisor, I changed my major to social work and added a minor in psychology. I loved this combination. I loved my classes, the content, and the idea of helping others.

After graduating, I stopped working in our family business and secured a position as a social worker at Cornerstone Services in Joliet. I began to recognize that I loved the work I was doing but did not like it when I had to close a case and never have contact with that client again. At about that same time, my dad asked me to return to work at our family business as the businesses were growing and they needed help. I knew the work; I knew how to sew, reupholster furniture, make mattress borders, manage the office, and how to work with people. And I enjoyed working with our family, so I decided to return to work full-time for the family business.

The businesses thrived, especially Pattern Designers, our quilting company. However, just over a decade later, competitive pricing for mattress manufacturing slowly began to hurt our small family business. Mattress stores were opening all over, selling big name brands like Sealy, Serta, Simmons, and Tempur-Pedic. We eventually realized we could no longer compete, so our family decided to close Royal Comfort, our mattress factory. My grandma went back to doing upholstery out of her home, and my grandpa continued to work for Pattern Designers, making deliveries. At the end of 1996, after nearly two decades, we closed the doors on our Michigan Avenue shop. I decided to take this opportunity to find another position for myself. Leaving the family business was difficult, but it was something I felt was necessary for my family, and the timing seemed appropriate.

By this time, my high school sweetheart and I were married and had two children. Our daughter had arrived in August 1989 and our son almost two years later. After we closed Royal Comfort, I started substitute teaching kindergarten through high school in schools across Will County. From that work, I realized I loved working in education. I loved helping students learn new material and watching their eyes light up after they struggled to learn a new concept—that ah-ha moment when the light bulb finally went on. I often wondered if this was how my grandma felt after she taught me how to measure, cut, and sew something. To know that I could be that someone who helped them learn something new felt gratifying.

After three months as a substitute teacher, I decided to head out to Lewis University again—not to return to school but to see about getting a new job within an educational setting that I already knew I loved. I began my work at Lewis as a secretary within the Career Education Program (LUCEP), now known as the School for Graduate, Professional, and Continuing Education (SGPCE). That was April 14, 1997. Since then, some of the other positions I have held at Lewis include Data Processing Assistant, Help Desk Coordinator/Assistant Director of Instructional Technology, Assistant Director of Teaching, Learning, & Technology (TLT), Student Success and Technology Specialist, and Student Success Coordinator. While none of these roles were actual social worker positions, they each included working with and supporting other people. My current role is Assistant Director, Programming, within Academic Services. This position is all about creating and enhancing academic programs as well as supporting members of our community in academic and technology-related ways. While working, I also pursued a master's degree at Lewis in Organizational Leadership with concentrations in Organizational Change and Training and Development. Although I have held a few different positions during my time at Lewis University, one thing has always remained the same: my passion for understanding and supporting others.

While each position I held at Lewis was fulfilling, I still wanted more. It was always my dream to move up and eventually into an administrative position, as a director or Assistant Dean. I thought that is what I had been called to do. I wanted to keep moving up, the way my grandma had. She went from working for others to having others work for

her. I wanted that for me, and I wanted to be able to contribute financially to support my family the way my grandma had always supported all of us. My grandma taught me that I could achieve my dreams through hard work and dedication. She also taught me that supporting my family wasn't just about keeping a roof over their head, having food, a car, or designer clothes, but that spending time with them was the best support I could provide. I always loved learning, and I realized I longed for more flexibility in my work schedule. To achieve my dream, I decided to pursue a doctorate. I completed a doctorate from Northern Illinois University, in Higher Education Leadership, defending my dissertation on March 9, 2020. While pursuing my doctorate, I was called in a new direction: I was set on securing a full-time professor position. This type of position would offer much more flexibility than a Monday through Friday, 8:30-5:00 position. It would allow me to be more available for my children and grandchildren, much like my grandma was always there to support her children and grandchildren. Owning her own business offered her scheduling flexibility to always be there if someone needed her. I realized this is what I truly wanted.

I was open to the idea of a full-time teaching position within the College of Business, as I have been an adjunct instructor teaching the Computer Applications and the Information Systems course since 2000, or teaching within the Organizational Leadership Program, which is what I obtained my master's degree in. I was also open to the idea of teaching within the College of Humanities, Fine Arts and Communications, as I recently began teaching within the Department of Communications. I thought everything was going as I had dreamt and even planned. Then, COVID-19 hit. In March 2020, one week after successfully defending my dissertation, we all began working remotely. I graduated in May 2020, but there were no full-time teaching positions available in my field. It was okay though, because I loved my role (at the time) as a Student Success Coordinator, responsible for the Success Scholars Program and, among many other things, providing academic technology support to all Lewis students. I was not in a rush to change positions, especially while the world was in turmoil.

Then, in May 2021, my life was shattered when a tragic car accident took the lives of my six-year-old grandson, Levi, and my daughter-in-law, Sara. Life as I knew it had changed forever. We are devastated. It was and continues to be hard. I am doing everything I can to support my son, Jonathan, and his two young daughters, Brooklyn and Dakota. The girls were both in the car at the time of the accident. The youngest was critically injured, and after four surgeries and lots of therapy, she has almost completely recovered, physically.

The oldest was treated for her injuries and soon released. Neither of them, Jonathan, nor any of us will ever fully recover mentally or emotionally from this tragedy. My daughter, Ryan, my son-in-law, Matt, and my other granddaughters, Payton, Elena, and Thea, all still struggle with this loss every single day as well.

Something like this tragedy puts everything into perspective, and your life-long journey becomes much clearer. I want to be like my grandma. I want to be present for my children and grandchildren like my grandma always was for me. I want to provide the love and support my family needs. I want to be the person my granddaughters look up to. I want to be the grandma my grandson can be proud of from heaven. I want to be that person students and coworkers can come to when they have questions. I want my family, especially my children and grandchildren, my students, and even those I work with to remember that life may be hard, we may hit bumps along the way, we may even have to take detours, but life is not all bad. We just have to take one day at a time. Some days, we might only take one hour or one minute at a time, but together, as a family or as a community, we can get through anything— just like my extraordinary grandma did so many times with her family and those around her.

Building a Better Life

by Antonieta S. Fitzpatrick, M.A.

Assistant Vice President for Student Success

As a kid, I didn't understand the outlook for children of high school dropouts, but my parents did. My parents worked long hours. Consequently, we didn't have regular family dinners, they weren't in the PTA, or at my track meets. And they didn't help me with my homework. I did have three older sisters, and they filled in some of those parenting gaps. On occasion, they'd help with homework or help me put together a cute outfit for the next day of school. They also were part of what kept my parents busy. My oldest sister had developmental disabilities and was dependent on my parents for many things. My other two sisters had wild streaks and often found themselves getting in trouble. My parents' plate was always full.

On the weekends, my mom would head to work and leave behind a long list of chores on the back of an old, tattered envelope: Vacuum, empty the bathroom garbage cans, dust, clean the mirrored closet doors. Chores were the worst part of my weekend, but we all had to do our part at home. I hated the sound of the vacuum so much that I would run it up and down the carpet, but never turn it on. The lines the vacuum left behind always fooled my mom. The highlight of the weekends were Sundays when most of us were home, and my dad would make breakfast ... waking up to the smell of chorizo and eggs and tortillas browning on the stove, finding my way to the kitchen to the sight of my dad cooking and watching *Soul Train*. After breakfast, we'd take a ride to St. Mary's Cemetery at 87th and Pulaski. Once we arrived, we all knew the routine: Clean up the grass, wipe the headstones, and then stand quietly and say our prayers for our Grandma and Grandpa Molinar.

Even though my parents worked long hours, there were many family traditions that tied our family closely together. For Christmas Eve, we would make dozens of tamales and sit around the table together enjoying a traditional Mexican meal, with everything homemade by us as a family— tamales, chicken and mole, rice and beans, tostadas, chips. And some years, we even made beautiful, bright pink, sweet tamales. Easters were spent in Chinatown with an early lunch and walking the shops on Wentworth. My dad would always drive us past the apartment he once called home. And once a month, we'd go to 26th street to collect rent, get some Mexican bread, and drive through the "old neighborhood." When I was in kindergarten, we moved from the Gage Park neighborhood in Chicago to the suburbs. To my parents, the move was a major accomplishment and a huge step towards what they would call "building a better life" for our family. I could always sense the pride my parents felt in these moments. It was important for them to stay connected to their roots and even more important for them to show us where our family started. These traditions and experiences are a big part of who I am today.

The other moments that stand out from being a kid are the times my sisters and I got in trouble. My parents were old-school, and our punishments included tabasco, jalapeños, soap in our mouth, and even the belt. I can still hear the sound of my dad's belt coming off. In the fourth grade, I remember progress report time, and that year was not my best. My parents expected us to do well in school, so rather than show them my bad grades, I decided to forge my mom's signature. I turned the signed report into my teacher, and it wasn't long before she realized what I had done. She called home, and I found myself in big trouble. Also, in the sixth grade, I decided to let a boy I liked sign the side of my shoes. I thought

he liked me, so I was so excited to have his autograph with me forever! When my dad saw my shoes, he was furious that I would deface myself in that way. And I remember my sisters getting in trouble for staying out past curfew, getting speeding tickets, or being out with boys they shouldn't have been out with.

Every time we got in trouble, not only did we get one of those old-school punishments, but we also got a lecture that reminded us of what our parents wanted for us—a better life, one that included an education which would then lead us to a job, a career, financial stability, and the ability to provide for our own families—something to be proud of, something that would make all their sacrifices worth it. To this day, I can still hear them saying, "We have worked so hard to provide you a life full of opportunities, how could you do this?" At times, this was hard to take in. I couldn't understand how, for example, letting a boy write on my shoe would derail my future. I was just a kid, but my parents had the highest of standards when it came to our behavior. They expected us to behave in a way that would not only lead to that better life, but they also expected us to represent our family and ourselves well.

The world judged my dad by his brown skin, his dark hair, his Mexican identity—and he knew it. On top of that, my parents were a biracial couple on the South Side of Chicago in the early 1970s. They faced criticism, judgement, and prejudice by strangers and family members alike. As I look back now,

I see how my parents tried to counter all of this by focusing on the things they could control—looking their best, their work ethic, integrity, reliability, honesty—and these were things they thought were important for us, too. Each action we took, each decision we made, even how we dressed and cared for ourselves—it was important to make our family proud. They always reminded us that one poor decision could very easily derail our future.

And when my parents talked about our future, they meant one thing: our education. They had no clue how college worked or the type of hard work it takes to get there, but they expected it of us. They learned the value of education by going through life without one.

My parents were sixteen and seventeen when they found out they were expecting my oldest sister. They dropped out of high school and found jobs—my dad at a meat packing company and my mom waiting tables. Over the next nine years, my sisters and I were born. My father eventually earned his GED and became a proud Teamster, driving semi-trucks for U.S. Foods. My mom found her way from waiting tables to becoming an Account Executive in the makeup and fragrance industry. My parents did whatever they could to provide for us and together built a beautiful life for our family. They made mistakes along the way, and certainly their punishments may not be socially acceptable today. Ultimately, though, through all the ups and downs, they ended up instilling strong values in

us—values like hard work, the importance of family, the importance of taking pride in yourself, and being true to your word. And, of course, the value of education.

As an adult and someone who works in higher education, I hear colleagues talk about the problems first-generation college students face in reaching academic success. I believe there is sometimes a tone of deficiency when talking about first-generation students, and ideas often center around how we might "get" the students "up to speed" in one way or another. As a first-gen college grad myself, I often reflect on my own experience. *How did I find success? What challenges did I face? How did I do it?*

Finding my way into college was not easy. I was fortunate to be at a high school where going to college was the norm. I followed the lead of my best friends. I knew if they were working on college applications, I needed to. If they were studying for the ACT, I needed to. And if they were visiting colleges, I needed to as well. I didn't know where I wanted to go to college but ended up choosing Illinois State University (ISU) with one of my best friends. Knowing I wouldn't be alone was a major relief. I will never forget move-in day. My dad loved getting to use his skills as a truck driver to have the most tightly and perfectly packed car around. When we pulled up outside my residence hall, he was ready to unload the car, just like he unloaded countless semi-trucks full of groceries. I could sense the pride he had, not only in his packing and unloading skills, but also in me, as his first daughter to head off to college.

The beginning of my first semester was filled with excitement. I was living with my best friend and was free from the strict rules of my parents. I went to my first college parties and made new friends from places I had never heard of. Things started to feel different, however, once classes settled in. As time went on, I couldn't seem to get my feet on the ground academically. I didn't know how to study, and I never felt like I was being a college student "right." I was in college because there was no other option. My parents expected me to go to college and graduate, and so there I was, trying to make it happen. I made it through my first semester but wasn't feeling optimistic about my classes for the spring.

Outside of classes, things were going well. My Resident Assistant, Kyle, encouraged me to apply to be an R.A. for the following schoolyear. I didn't feel like I had the leadership potential for the position, but Kyle's encouragement gave me the push I needed. Aside from that, having room and board paid for would bring my family some financial relief. Before I knew it, I was selected to be an R.A. My self-doubt subsided long enough to allow me to celebrate the good news, but soon enough, I was sensing the position was going to be out of reach for me. My spring grades came in, and I was on academic probation. Not only was I at risk of being dismissed from the university, but I also lost the R.A. position. The news was devastating and confirmed my feelings of not

doing college "right." All I could think about was my parents. How would I be able to tell them this news? I was the one in our family that made it to college, the one that would graduate college and build a better life.

I never told my parents or anyone else. I didn't want to have to explain what happened. I worried others would doubt me in all the ways I was doubting myself that first year. Somewhere in the midst of all the devastation and self-doubt, I knew there was no possible way I was going to give up. All those childhood lectures from my parents re-played in my head. I imagined myself walking across the graduation stage with my parents and sisters watching. While the self-doubt remained, I was absolutely determined. I brushed myself off and came up with a plan to get back on track.

I came home that summer and took classes at the community college. I told my family I wanted to go to school somewhere closer to home. My dad had been delivering groceries and supplies to the cafeteria at Saint Xavier for years. During that time, he got to know the cook, Gomez, really well. When I mentioned being closer to home, he said, "Go talk to Gomez, mija. He will help you." My dad couldn't help me with very much related to college, but he did help me by connecting me with Gomez. So, of course, my first stop when I visited Saint Xavier was the kitchen. Gomez immediately felt like family. It was clear he had been hearing about me and my sisters from my dad over the years. Soon enough, the devastation of my first year was behind me, and I was

> *I love my work, but the work I hold closest to my heart is working with our first-generation students and our students who are on academic probation. I do everything I can to help them see themselves as not just college students but college graduates.*

getting settled at Saint Xavier. Classes were hard, but the challenges of my first year gave me motivation to ask for help when I needed it. I tried different ways of studying. I spent more time in the quiet of the library. I was more focused on what I wanted because I knew what it felt like to have it almost slip away.

After not too long at Saint Xavier, I became a Student Ambassador for the Office of Admissions. Then I started seeing fliers posted about becoming a Resident Assistant. I wanted to apply but felt nervous about the thought of losing the position again. I really wanted to live on campus, so I decided to go for it. I was lucky to be hired, especially as a commuter student, and before I knew it, I felt like I had the hang of things. I had a great group of friends I could lean on, I had the support and guidance of staff members and eventually worked on building connections with some faculty members, too. After all those thoughts and feelings of not doing college right, I graduated from Saint Xavier with 3.4 GPA and a double major in Organizational Communication and Spanish. The day I graduated was incredible—it was that moment I imagined. It was a bright, sunny day, and I was dressed in a perfectly pressed, black gown and matching cap. My parents were beaming with pride from the stands. My mom was holding a beautiful bouquet of pastel-colored flowers. I could see my sisters, my two little nephews, and Joe Fitzpatrick, my longtime boyfriend, waiting for me to cross the stage. After the ceremony, we went home for a big graduation party in the backyard and, of course, an amazing spread of homemade Mexican food.

After graduation, I moved home and found a job in advertising sales. Things were good, but the work wasn't fulfilling or inspiring. Something was missing. At that time, I started considering going back to school for my master's degree. The funny thing is I wasn't even sure what I wanted to study, yet something was drawing me back to higher education. I started researching my options and was quite lucky to get a Graduate Assistant position in Residence Life at Saint Xavier. My time as a grad assistant allowed me to continue to work with some wonderful professionals—the same professionals who helped me when I was struggling as an undergrad, including Gomez. In working with them, I realized that I could make a career out of helping students just like me. Looking back now, my career was right in front of me all along. I just didn't see it.

Today, I am fortunate to have served as Lewis' Director of Academic Services in the Center for Academic Success and Enrichment and now as Assistant Vice President for Student Success. In my roles, I work with a team of incredible staff to support students' academic and post-graduation goals. I love my work, but the work I hold closest to my heart is working with our first-generation students and our students who are on academic probation. I do everything I can to help them see themselves as not just college students but college graduates. I try to be for them what I needed during those difficult times in college. I give them a safe space to share the feelings that come along with being on probation. I make sure they are connected to people and programs on campus that will remind them of their strengths and talents. I spend time talking with them about things other than their academic progress—hobbies, TV shows, family and friends, sports and current events, favorite recipes and even pets! Eventually, I help my students come to understand that one difficult semester is not a reason to give up on their dream of graduating from college.

The other aspect of my work that I am most passionate about is identifying and working to remove and eliminate all the things we, as institutions of higher education, put in the way of our students' success. Higher education theorist and researcher Vincent Tinto puts it perfectly when he says, "To be serious about student success, institutions would recognize that the roots of attrition lie not only in their students and the situations they face, but also in the very character of the educational settings, now assumed to be natural in higher education, in which they ask students to learn" (Tinto 5). In my work now, I think back to my days at Illinois State and losing my R.A. position. Student leadership positions are often reserved for students with above a 2.5 GPA—a rule and standard set by countless universities. In higher education, we know these types of positions lead to student growth and connection to community, and yet we have established a rule that keeps these positions out of reach for students who may benefit the most. What if, for example, there was a program that could have provided academic support while also allowing me to gain the leadership development and university connections that come along with an R.A. position? I think I would have flourished and, based on my academic stumble and first-generation, Mexican identity, would have become an empathetic, impactful leader in the residence halls. Instead, I left ISU altogether. Luckily, I found my home at Saint Xavier, and eventually all those ups and downs led me to where I am today.

Works Cited

Tinto, Vincent. "Taking Retention Seriously: Rethinking the First Year of College."*NACADA Journal*, Fall, Vol. 19, No. 2, 1999, pp. 5-9. http://dx.doi.org/10.12930/0271-9517-19.2.5

Confront Failure to Blaze Your Personal, Hope-Filled Life Path

by John Greenwood, Ph.D.

Professor *Emeritus*, Department of Psychology (Retired)

What's that? You think you already **have** *hope and have always been told to* **avoid** *failure. You say you feel you are here to be educated, not to find meaning. Welcome to the dark fun-house escape room of the rest of your life. I want to share the corkscrewed, roller-coaster story of my journey. Perhaps by seeing my experiences, you can find your way more easily. I want you to begin the search for your own personal, purpose-driven life of meaning and hope. I urge you to accept the impact of the jump scares of events you can't escape. Accept that you will face "failures" but can overcome and learn from them. Doing so creates the necessary, redeeming force to adapt, improvise, and overcome sink holes on your path to purpose. Use your superpower to destroy "failures" by redefining them as "lessons" to learn. Few face the burdens of Congressman John Lewis or Senator Tammy Duckworth, but all our lives are filled with struggles, pain, and failure that we face and overcome. I offer my early life and hard lessons to build a life of meaning and purpose. Your path is your path, but these lessons may help you persist on that path.*

My home was stable, with both parents and an older brother, in an extremely rural, Iowa farming area on the Mississippi, called Pleasant Valley. For the first several years, I went to a small school, with outdoor privies (toilets) ... got a bit intense in the winter. The teacher used old-style methods like chalkboards and mimeograph worksheets she made (all teachers were women). "Good students" helped by erasing boards and clapping erasers. Most students were farmers' or workers' kids with parents without college experience. A farmer's feedlot was our playground. My classmates were not rich, but they were good people and good citizens.

My parents were educated. My father graduated from University of Illinois and was an executive at ALCOA Aluminum. We moved from Ohio to Iowa when his team built ALCOA's biggest factory. My parents were part of the elite set in the nearby metro area. We lived in the Valley. On the river bluff, above the Valley, was a core of millionaires with the real juice in the area. The country club was there, and we were members. The tension between these two cultures defined my life.

I ran into my first "failure" immediately. Ohio didn't teach reading in primary school, but they did in the Valley. The teachers found out and set me back to learn to read. So, I flunked kindergarten! It wasn't my fault, or anyone's, but I felt like I had failed. I felt like a dummy. I reacted by becoming a reader. After the usual "Dick and Jane" books, I moved to fantasy and sci-fi. That helped me deal with loneliness and gave me a world I could control. It triggered imagination and brought me new worlds. My expanded vocabulary became my major tool for thinking and understanding. *My point here is that "failure" can come in many ways, earned or accidental, but the threat to your sense of your identity and confidence can be powerful. Early events can be powerful, especially when they are tied to valued aspects of your culture. These events are inevitable and inescapable. They shaped my social patterns, sense of who I was, and my self-worth. On the other hand, I responded in a manner that was ultimately of great value and a new source of worth, pleasure, and sense of purpose. I had started on my path toward my ultimate vocation in higher education. You can do that, too.*

"As the twig is bent, so grows the tree." The Valley folk knew we were culturally different. My home was filled with classical music, mixed with popular music, including my favorite—the Gershwin folk-opera, "Porgy and Bess"—as well as other popular music, especially Latino music. There was art on the walls and a well-stocked library. My mother was a political and community leader in the nearby Quad Cities and a leader in the Valley women's group (the Grit Club) working to improve the Valley. Our home was a sanctuary for international students from local colleges, mostly Latino but also from Africa, Europe, and Asia. Kids from the city's settlement house, where my mother volunteered, came to the house regularly. These were the few "foreigners" who came anywhere near the Valley. I never knew anything different, and they were all welcome in our house. I knew that I came from a different culture and felt very ignorant of the wider world.

It was weird when I went to the country club. I used the pool, but the rich kids knew I was from the Valley and shunned me. When I started to caddy (carrying golf bags), the caddies and caddy master knew I was a member, so they didn't know what to do with me. So, from the start, I was on the outside looking in, not abused, just "other," not fitting in anywhere. It would seem strange to be lonely when surrounded by people, but I was. *Some of you may feel that way at Lewis. I chose to lie low, but you should reach out, to just a few and then to more. It takes strength, but you can find out what you share with them.*

My mother enrolled me in the city junior high. I had to be bused to the school. I was isolated, joining a group of kids who had been together all their lives. I didn't fit in, but it was a better school. I was a smart kid and a hard worker in an exciting environment. I was placed in the "college-prep" track rather than the "voc-ed" one, which defined social groups. I had NO clue what to do with my life but knew college was required. I worked in the fields and factory and didn't want that. I connected to the science faculty, who were doing the neat stuff—dissecting frogs, and such. They helped me and saw I was a top student. The "sorting hat" of the school had made its choice. *Be open and reach out to things you like.*

I bonded with the physics teacher, the best teacher I ever had. Due to the Cold War and Space Race, the federal government developed a new science curriculum. My physics teacher remodeled all the courses and equipment. I volunteered to help him. I really enjoyed the physical demos, like water wave tables and diffraction experiments. I decided to become a "nuclearphysicist" (one word for me) because of his interest in me and because it seemed high status. I helped form a science club called the "Mesons." Seeds of being an educator had been planted, though I was not aware of that. *Let your enthusiasm build a base for path choices.*

These social bonds illustrate my next point. At critical periods in your life, facing confusion and doubt, the social context becomes powerful. Supportive teachers and a group of like-minded friends provide a support and mentoring system that helps you overcome fears and shaky esteem. You become part of a quasi-family that is powerful in impact, even if brief. They may become anchors later as you realize how much you shared. Older mentors are very important since they aren't obliged to support you, as you feel parents must do. We are not built to be loners but can become that. The key is to know and seek healthy support. We need to reach out for those people. So many find new paths after finding someone who believes in them. The wise choice of others is often the hardest part.

I went out for sports teams—first baseball, then track and wrestling, and finally football. I had no training, late growth, and limited early success. I went out for football when I grew tall and big. Before my senior year, I went through the summer two-day practices to get ready. I felt good being part of the team. It was a state-ranked team, and I enjoyed belonging to a high-status jock group. Then another of those crossroads came up. The Vice Principal brought me in and said I needed to make a choice. He said I had a chance for scholarships and entry to good schools but only if I dropped football to focus on classes. He was an authority figure, representing the "educated class," but I really liked sports. I decided to drop football just before the season started. The coach really got pissed, calling me a loser and quitter. It really hurt as well as put

> **"**
>
> While events happen that shift everything and are seldom under your control, they create opportunities. The key is what you do with them.
>
> **"**

me on the outside again. It also left a deep desire for sports as a source of redemption that emerged later. I graduated with super high test scores and lots of scholarships. I was accepted to several top schools. I chose Carnegie Tech and planned to room with my best friend from the Mesons nerd group. *I made the choice, as you will, but it may leave scars.*

Well, then, I was all set! Except my father refused to fill out the financial aid forms, so that left only a full-ride Naval ROTC scholarship. Carnegie didn't have NROTC, but Iowa State University (ISU) did. Iowa State was also top notch in physics and closer to home, but without my friend. "Moo U" felt like another disappointment.

We are finally at your stage of life. ISU was a big place with thousands of students and programs, spread out over hell's half acre. I did well enough in classes though they were mega-sized classes without interaction. We lived in single-sex dorms with other confused, immature students with no restrictions. The dorms were organized in "houses," which were like frats with lots of intramural activities, meaning sports!

I was on several dorm teams, even winning the wrestling title one year. I also joined the school's soccer team, without experience, but with enthusiasm. I was the only American on the team, but I was comfortable with all the international players because of my childhood. I also was on the school's judo team, leaning on my wrestling background. I even won a conference championship. Then there was the semi-pro basketball team I was on. Surprise! My grades slipped. *We naturally tend to move toward short-term activities that bring a sense of value and acceptance, even if we "know" that we should be thinking about long term goals. Your toughest choice is to pick adult acts over the fun stuff.*

I enjoyed sports, but I found core classes pointless. They focused on math, not physics in a concrete sense. I could do it, but it wasn't what I wanted. There were few labs, just blackboards with equations. I was interested in *using* physics, not the theory. There was no advisement since the classes were locked-in sequences. Classes were ten-week quarters with up to seven classes a term, so it was a constant battle to keep up. I recently found old class notes, and they were filled with sketches of students and teachers. I was already showing more interest in people than equations. I slipped more and more, flunking some classes. I retook and passed them but didn't really care. I had no mentors and no guidance. I was blindly coasting and without a GPS. *Lack of guidance is often why so many new students end up dropping out.*

Finally, as a senior, I flunked out! Talk about your failure experience! I went home and got a job in the ALCOA factory. Not a good time—back in the Valley, without friends, and facing my parents every day as they tried to be supportive. I was in the best shape of my life, physically, but in a really dark headspace. I knew I had to go back and finish "something" with no clue what I wanted. I was at a crossroads, with no road signs. I had to work it out on my own, dealing with humiliation and a profound sense of failure. It could have gone badly. The "grit" to move forward depended on willingness to accept the past and act, despite the head fog. It was a time to be honest and not live in a "pity party."

I completed purgatory and applied for re-entry to Iowa State. I had worked out four different degree plans, based on different majors. It turned out that I parked closest to the psychology office and went there first. A bored graduate student was there, working as a Teaching Assistant/ Advisor, and so I became a psych major! It was my most interesting area, so it wasn't totally random, but close. I took all psych classes and finished in one year. Again, there was no advisement. I ended with a 2.25 GPA despite getting virtually all As in the psych classes. *Notice that tiny events can have a major impact. We must face them, commit, and make them work, despite the*

uncertainty. You will find more strength with each step up.

In the last term, I took several grad classes to "prove myself." I knew grad school was essential but only applied to ISU. I had super GRE test scores, but there was that 2.25 GPA. Predictably, ISU was a selective school and turned me down. Bam! Back on that foggy road again with no path, not even a crossroad—no skills, no job experience, and no direction. *Realize that outside forces shape decisions even if you don't know it. The world was turbulent at that time. Like distant lightning, I was vaguely aware of events, but only saw my own confusion. Flunking out changed my life. It may even have saved it, since I did not receive the Marine commission I had earned in the Marine Option of NROTC! Most of my friends ended up in Viet Nam. I completed my obligation in the inactive reserves. My point is that your lives are always under the winds of powerful, external events that shape or determine your path. These storms often cannot be anticipated, fully understood, or even recognized but will change your life path in monumental ways.*

My high school friend was doing a med school residency in California. It was the 60s, I had a car, so I chose to go out to see him. Why not? It was time to be a hippy for a while. I couldn't even get an hourly gig! My friend was busy and living with his soon-to-be wife. Talk about a fifth wheel! I sat on the bank of the Sacramento River and pondered what the hell to do with my life.

Pondering didn't help and was depressing. In late summer, I just decided to take off, to go to Idaho to visit my brother. He was working on his geology Ph.D. in Moscow, Idaho. It was not a happy option for me, since we had not been close, and he was a success in all ways that matter—the older son who had "made it." I was just wandering and looking for someone who would let me in, despite the shame that I would feel. I arrived in August with no plan or great hope.

Here is where I want to reemphasize a key factor that you must accept and deal with. While events happen that shift everything and are seldom under your control, they create opportunities. The key is what you do with them. We talk about luck—but accept that these events will happen and will change your life. You have to recognize them and accept them. Most importantly, you have to act and find short term goals until the fog clears a bit. The first step is hard but builds momentum for moving.

In my case, my brother was welcoming. That was nice. It felt good to be valued as a brother. *Remember, that family—biological or social—is always the foundation for strength.* Well, he asked, "Why don't you go to grad school?" I thought he was joking, but he wasn't. He always was a doer, not a talker, and started the process. He approached his own school's master's program in psych. Though it was less than two weeks before classes began, they let me in, based mostly on my high GRE score.

See what I mean about luck? The accident of timing, my semi-random wandering, and the strength of my brother created a path! Now came my part. I had to carry MY load. I worked hard and made it work. I completed the program in one year, including a research thesis. I was intense in committing to the work. I was NOT going to screw this up. I enjoyed the content and found research fascinating. That energy shaped the patience and determination for this drive for redemption and recovery of a sense of value and purpose. I had finally found a meaningful path!

OK ... Now what? Time to move on from Idaho, but where, and to what? I applied to several grad schools in social psych. I was really excited about finally dealing with real world research that could have an impact. I got into several doctoral programs and picked the one that gave a full ride and stipend, in Buffalo, New York. I finished my thesis and drove from Idaho to New York without focusing on anything but the road. I had little idea what would happen but had new faith that I could deal with it. I had found a vocation that would become the anchor for the rest of my life. Increasingly, my concern for people brought commitment to teaching, advising students, and using my professional knowledge to push for social justice and for building strong organizational systems.

The final shaping force has been sharing three decades with the Lasallian Christian Brothers. The Lasallian mission gave me a formal framework to make sense of my life. *Lewis is a true nurturing, mission-based community that cares most about your personal growth. I urge you to seek out the* opportunities, listen to the Brothers, and find doors to service that will give your life meaning after Lewis. You will learn new skills, but what is most important is to learn new meanings that become the spine steel that will let you "get behind the mule in the morning and plow," even when there is thunder in the air.

I hope you recognize the key lessons I have tried to share. You will find the world scary and confusing. Accept that as a fact to be faced. Find friends who support you, especially when you're struggling. You need mentors who help you clarify your dreams and are models for your actions. Accept the fact, even the need, to embrace failure as the price of success. Redefine it as a hard lesson. Make an endless wish, and act, despite the pain and fear. You can do it alone, but you don't need to if you look for kindred spirits. You will slowly work out the impact of your past in shaping or limiting your dreams. Most importantly, you must find a source of value in your life. May each day bring you more joy and hope on your journey.

Feeling Alone: You are Not Alone

by Morris Jenkins, J.D., Ph.D.

Associate Professor, Department of Justice, Law, and Public Safety Studies (Retired)

As Frank Sinatra sang, "Regrets, I've had a few/But then again, too few to mention ... I did it my way...."

Thinking about my past brings up a lot of good thoughts and a few thoughts that were painful. I chose to describe a few of the "not-so-nice" situations. I believe that these painful situations got me to where I am now. I have been blessed to have a fruitful academic career as a faculty member and mid-level administrator. This, coupled with my brief foray into a legal arena, makes me smile when I look back on my life. As a faculty member or dean, I have had many experiences around the challenging issues of diversity, equity, and inclusion with faculty, staff and student bodies at predominately white institutions (PWI). I am writing this piece from the perspective of "other," or outsider, in these situations. I hope this writing inspires other individuals who may also have the feeling of being the outsider. This feeling can be real and/or perceived. And the feeling can be influenced by outside factors, such as bias and systemic discrimination.

These obstacles can be impediments that can be conquered—by going over, under, or through them. I want to emphasize: The feeling is just a feeling, and one that can be overcome.

I was born and raised in Detroit, Michigan, the oldest child of three and the only boy. My father and mother came to Detroit to work in the automobile and other car-related industries. They were afforded employment opportunities not available to them in their native South Carolina. During my childhood, the city of Detroit was not the "Chocolate City" that it is today. My neighborhood was composed of Black people who hailed from the South and individuals straight out of Poland. In fact, during my grammar and high school days, I knew only a few individuals whose parents were born in Detroit. My neighborhood was full of "immigrants" who came to the city to work in the various jobs related to the automobile industry. Early in my life, I was aware of racial discrimination, but it was based on my experiences in the South with White folk in my parents' home state of South Carolina. Of course, in Detroit, we had problems with law enforcement—they constantly called me and my Black friends the "N-word" and my Polish friends the "dumb P-word"—but they abused all the young men regardless of race and ethnicity.

During my primary and high school years, Detroit was in the middle of social upheaval that culminated in the Detroit Rebellion in July 1967. The rebellion was sparked by police abuse that impacted most of the young people in Detroit. After the rebellion, it triggered White and Black flight to the suburbs. After 1967, the social dynamics in the city went through drastic changes. The relationship was strained between the youth of Detroit and law enforcement all through the 1960s.

My respite from some of the social madness occurred in my elementary school, Davison Elementary. There, I was considered one of the high achievers, and I, along with my classmates, received an abundance of support from the teachers and staff at the school. They prepared us for the real world. I found out later in life that I scored some high marks on an IQ test, so I was double-promoted and was given opportunities to participate in many special academic programs around the city. One of the programs I was chosen for—an after-school program at a school outside of my neighborhood—gave me my first tangible experience with the dynamics of racism.

I already felt like a fish out of water in the program's neighborhood given some of the different cultural issues there compared with my own Davison neighborhood. For example, my neighborhood was composed of Black people with roots from the South and White people whose roots were from Poland. Students in this new program were White but not from Poland. In my own neighborhood, all of us basically ate the same foods: a high dose of pork, donuts (or Polish Paczkis) and salt-based foods. During one of the program sessions in this other neighborhood, the teacher asked us what we wanted for snacks, and all the other kids stated they wanted a pizza pie. They asked me whether I would like one, and I timidly said sure. I had no idea what pizza was. I was thinking it was going to be a sweet potato pie or a pie that was popular with my Polish friends. I was very surprised to see this pie with tomato sauce and cheese, but the sausage did remind me of good food from my 'hood. During this time in the special program, we also shared different types of music we enjoyed. In my neighborhood, the predominant forms of music were the blues, jazz, Motown, and Polka. The kids from the program's neighborhood were into a group called The Beatles, a group I never heard about at the time. I felt a little apprehension in this program, but these students tried to make me comfortable.

My negative experience did not occur in the actual program but in the program's neighborhood. Because the program was a few miles from my neighborhood, I had to be dropped off and picked up at the school. After the program, I would stand outside of the school for about a half-hour waiting on either my mother or father to pick me up. One evening while I was waiting, a group of boys and young men spotted me. In my ten-year-old eyes, these guys appeared to be sixteen years and older. While waiting, the kids started yelling at me to go home, and for the first time I was called the N-word by individuals who were not police or Klansmen in the South. For the first time in my young life, I felt fear. As I was trying to deal with this group, I smelled the pungent odor of what I later found out to be tobacco and alcohol. To this day, whenever I smell cigarettes or booze, it takes me back to that day. I was roughed up a bit but tried to fight back the best that I could. Fortunately, I could run pretty fast and got away. I stayed in the bushes and waited for my parents to pick me up. I was a little disheveled and had a busted lip. I never told my father what really happened and just said I fell down playing a game of football with the other kids. In addition to being roughed up because of my race, this event was the first of many experiences of my being the only Black person, or one of the few Black persons, in various contexts.

The next major event occurred at Michigan State University (MSU). I was fortunate enough to be accepted at scores of colleges and universities. Most of the acceptances were academic ones, but a couple of them were athletic. I chose Michigan State over institutions such as MIT or Boston College. My parents didn't have a high school diploma and knew very little about colleges. They were just excited that I had a chance for free rides. At my first orientation at MSU, I was one of about six hundred new Black students that complemented the existing three hundred Black upper-class students. Little did we realize that we were almost a thousand students out of a student body of 50,000. Again, there was the culture shock. I met White students from all over the world. As a sixteen-year-old freshman, I was not only intimidated by some of the older students but felt out of place in this environment outside of Detroit.

During my time at MSU, there was a lot of self-segregation outside of the classroom. Blacks ate and partied with Blacks, Whites socialized with Whites, and the contingent of international students congregated in a separate dorm. Looking back, I can only imagine how the international students felt, surrounded by a bunch of young, wild and crazy Americans. Unlike my time in Detroit, where the "gang" was composed of Poles and Blacks that served as a support system, the support systems at MSU were generally all Black. There were Black fraternities and political organizations around campus. The one exception to this segregation occurred in April 1970. National Guardsman shot four students dead at Kent State in Ohio, and police killed two students at Jackson State in Mississippi. For a brief period of time that year, almost all students and some faculty were united against the oppression from the system and the Vietnam War.

After an "involuntary departure" from Michigan State (given that my major was

> **"**
> To a certain degree, all of us can be and probably are 'the other.' To all of you 'others' and outsiders: Keep on pushing.
> **"**

partying), I entered the U.S. Army. There were many young men and women from all types of racial and ethnic backgrounds, and that feeling of being the "only one" didn't occur in the Army. The United States Army, especially the unit I was assigned to, was a racially and ethnically diverse environment. However, there was a lot of racial and ethnic self-segregation outside of our time on duty. On the job, we all worked together; once we left the unit, we went our separate ways. Blacks socialized with Blacks; Latinos socialized with Latinos; Whites socialized with Whites. During this time, I served in West Germany, and there were times that we felt like "the other," but it was due to being an American more so than our racial and ethnic identities. My time there was very enjoyable, especially considering that I could have been in Vietnam.

After the Army, I decided to join the Marine Corps. (All I am going to say is that Scotch and Martinis can make a person do strange things.) They had all of us new Marine Corps recruits take a standardized test to determine which job we would do in the Corps. They made me take the test three times to ensure the score was right. Subsequently, I found out that I scored the highest points in my cohort. Because of my score, they placed me in a group that focused on avionics, one of the most desired occupations in the Corps. I was the only Black person in the cohort. I did not have a racial support group during this time. The social breakdowns were generally based upon preferences of music. The Country and Western folks hung together, the Hard Rockers were another group, and my group was composed of folks that liked disco or soul music. It was a very small group compared to the others, but we had each other's back whenever we went to town. We would not let the "townies" or the sailors from the Navy mess with any of us. The experience wasn't as traumatic as my experience in elementary school, but the feeling of not fitting in was apparent. The United States Marine Corps was very much different from the United States Army. Unlike in the Army, Black people and other People of Color were a distinct numerical minority in the Marine Corps. The environment was ripe for individual as well as institutional racism. In addition, my time with the USMC was in the United States, thus discrimination for being a United States citizen did not occur. However, within both military environments, the self-segregation tended to insulate us from the negative impact of institutional racism and actually helped create a sense of belonging.

After my two stints in the military, rather than go home to Detroit, I decided to go to South Carolina where I finished my bachelor's degree from Claflin College, a Historically Black College or University (HBCU). At Claflin, I was not a racial minority, but I was the only student at the school whose roots were from Detroit. However, even in a mono-racial environment, I was still feeling like the outsider. Being from the Midwest/North, made me stick out like a sore thumb. In a way, I felt I was perceived as not being Black. Many of the students felt that I talked "White" and some of the slang was much different from the slang we used in Detroit. One example that still sticks with me was the slang South Carolina Black people used to refer to White people. In Detroit, we referred to Whites as White and a few other derogatory terms. In South Carolina, White people were referred to as "buckras," which I subsequently found out was a derogatory term, even though it took me a couple of years to find that out.

Prior to graduation from Claflin, I was accepted for admission at Stetson University College of Law in St. Petersburg, Florida. I believe that all my previous experiences prepared me for my law school and graduate school experiences. Out of 140 students in my class, I was the only Black person. I later found out that I was only the thirteenth Black student to graduate from the oldest law school in the state of Florida. Much of the terminology used by my fellow students and their perceptions of society were different from mine. For example, I had a strong grasp of criminal law and, to a certain extent, constitutional law. Torts, property law, and contract law were foreign to me. However, after conversations with some of my White classmates, I found that they had very little knowledge of criminal law and felt lost with many of the concepts within criminal law. Today, I am still good friends with a few of the students from this group; we have a mini-reunion every ten years or so.

After graduating from Stetson and working for a few years in the legal profession, I decided to go for a Ph.D. and was accepted in a public policy program at Northeastern University in Boston. At that time, Boston was a hotbed of racial conflict. In my opinion, the environment in Boston was similar to that of South Carolina in the 1960s or to apartheid in South Africa in the pre-Mandela days. However, the University was insulated from some of the strife. I was one of two Black people in a cohort of fourteen students. This class was composed of men and women who already had successful careers and were getting the degree to enhance their careers: a successful lawyer who happened to also be a medical doctor; two individuals who had international government experiences; a young woman who worked with the governor of Massachusetts on healthcare policy; another young man who was an aide at the United Nations; and the other Black person was a man who was a mid-level administrator for the Boston Police Research and Evaluation section. He happened to be from Michigan and was a former trombone player for the Count Basie Band.

As we went around, each of us stated what we were going to do: become a high-level administrator, go into politics, do some work internationally … were some of the responses. By the time they got to me, I noticed one of the faculty members had a look of disgust and frustration on his face. I said I wanted to be a professor, and the face of the faculty member brightened up. He said, "At least one of you will enter a noble profession." From that point on, the feeling of being the outsider subsided. In fact, the wife of the other Black dude really thanked me for talking her husband into leaving his well-paid administrative position that was causing him health problems and going into the academy; he is now a community college president in Western Michigan.

I remember my father saying, "No man is an island." To a certain degree, all of us can be and probably are "the other." To all of you "others" and outsiders: Keep on pushing. I believe that we all should persevere through our internal feelings as well as the external obstacles that may impede progress. As a professor, I see some students who have internally based, and sometimes externally based, feelings of being the outsider. Their feelings could be based on such differences as race, color, sexual orientation, religion, or musical preference. *Just remember: You are not alone with these feelings.* And they can be overcome through internal fortitude coupled with reaching out to others for support.

What's crucial: Having more of the "others" in the academy and acknowledgement of some of these feelings by fellow academicians. The academy is at the vanguard of positive social change. As the current debate around critical race theory and other theories and paradigms that contradict the dominant Eurocentric, heterosexual, male, Christian-centered theoretical foundations rages, the voices of "the other" are needed to bring multiple perspectives in the teaching and research within the academy. Having more "outsiders" will help us to achieve the goals and objectives of our diversity efforts. I hope this piece inspires another "outsider" to come to the academy.

The Gift of Being Average

by Jung Kim, Ph.D.

Professor of Reading & Literacy
Co-chair, Department of Education

**Harvard-Bound ...
Or Not**

My halmoni's (grandmother's) dying wish was that I would go to Harvard. Spoiler, at the time, I was finishing my freshman year at the University of Illinois Urbana-Champaign and didn't transfer to Harvard. To be fair, I honestly don't think my halmoni knew the name of any other American university, but I still feel a twinge of sadness that I never attained that dream for her—not for undergrad, not for my master's, not for my Ph.D., and not for a place of employment. So many missed chances to triumphantly do that *one* thing for her. I honestly can't remember her asking me for anything else my whole life. I'm sure she probably did at some point, but nothing comes to mind. And so even in my forties, this memory still haunts me. But it also set a tone for how I grew up and how I struggled for so long with who or what I wanted to be. She, along with my parents, wanted me to do my best, and doing "my best" would mean I was at the top of my class, attend an Ivy League college, and become a lawyer or

a doctor (and they didn't mean the kind of doctor I currently am).

While attending smaller Catholic schools for K-8, I did well in school. We didn't really have rankings, but I pulled all As and received positive reviews at parent-teacher conferences. My move to public school— and from the suburbs of Philadelphia to the suburbs of Chicago—was a little rockier. Public school was much more competitive, and I was definitely a little fish in a big pond. Amongst the many transitions and "things learned" from that move, one thing became clear—that I was not particularly gifted in math ... or science. In high school, I was not in honors math and was scraping by with low Bs in honors science courses. In fact, I probably wouldn't have even gotten a B in Honors Chemistry without the help of my lab partner Ray, who quickly realized he would have to set up all the experiments if all the equipment was going to survive to the end of the class period intact (Thanks, Ray!).

I did well in English. I always loved to read and read voraciously as a kid, something my parents encouraged as they saw it as a road to higher academic achievement. Alas, it seemed to only manifest high academic achievement in English and maybe social studies. And what does one become when they're only really good at reading and writing? To my parents, the obvious answer was a lawyer. However, when my junior year English teacher talked about how a teacher encouraged *her* to be an English teacher, it got my wheels turning. Now, mind you, she did not encourage *me* to be an English teacher, just how *she* ended up going into teaching. And while I think most of my teachers liked me well enough in high school, none of them singled me out as having potential gifts or warranting special attention or encouragement. I was just another quiet Asian American kid that did "just fine."

High school was a struggle, then, constantly juggling my parents' very high expectations with my slightly above-average skill set. I did okay, but there were many late nights and freak-outs that still only brought me to being "okay." When it came to college applications, my parents wanted me to apply to only "brand name" (i.e., Ivy League or close to it) colleges. I ended up applying to many schools where my mildly successful grades and test scores did nothing to make me stand out, and so I ended up at my "safety," U of I. While I know it's an outstanding school, I felt a deep sense of shame for not being "good enough" for my parents. As the oldest, I felt all the hopes and expectations pinned on me by my parents to set an example for my younger siblings. And as an English major at a state school, I had dashed those hopes and expectations. After that, my parents shifted their dreams to my sister, who *did* end up pre-med at Yale University (although she too would end up the "wrong" kind of doctor, a veterinarian, but that's another story).

From that point on, my family wrote me off as the kid that would not excel. My sister went to two Ivy League universities—Yale and then the University of Pennsylvania (veterinarian)—and my brother went to Berkeley (engineer). The choices I would make and the convictions I had led me to a path different from theirs. I wasn't driven by grades and accolades in the same way that my siblings were or that my parents thought I should be. I wanted to make a difference in the world in immediate, localized ways. I found teaching to be the vehicle for this. After one last-ditch effort for me to apply to law school the night before my first day of teaching, they begrudgingly accepted teaching as acceptable. However, I continued to disappoint my parents as I chose to teach at a neighborhood high school on Chicago's West Side and not the affluent, competitive suburban schools they wanted.

It was my experiences in Chicago Public schools, though, and the massive systemic inequity I saw, that ultimately led me to pursue my master's and then my doctorate at University of Illinois Chicago (UIC). And not unlike my undergraduate applications, I had no clue how to choose or apply for doctoral programs. I was the first in my family to pursue an advanced degree. I ended up applying to UIC because it was close, had education programs, and some name recognition. This haphazard decision-making, though, would be a fortuitous one. The professors and classmates I had would further shape and deepen my commitment to equity and social justice.

"Good Enough"

It was during this time in graduate school that I heard an interview with Mark Bittman, the former *New York Times* food critic and food writer. In this interview, he talked about a myth that Americans had come to believe about cooking—that everything had to be amazing and gourmet or it wasn't worth your time. In contrast, he contended that Americans needed to embrace "good enough" as a motto for their cooking. While it was fun to make gourmet-fantastic meals, if fear of something not being amazing was what discouraged you from cooking at all, then "good enough" was a belief to be embraced.

While Bittman was talking about things like people being afraid of making pancakes from scratch, what I heard from him was permission to not being perfect and just being "good enough." So often in mainstream American culture, excellence is prized and only the best is demanded. Anything less than that is failure. In truth, this isn't sustainable. We can't give 110% all the time (and not just because it's mathematically impossible). It is not humanly possible to

give our all for every single endeavor in our lives. Nor can the only measuring stick be "all or nothing." Yet, that is the stick by which I had been measured growing up, and the stick by which I was still using to beat myself with for not being good enough. And I was drowning in my sense of failure, overwhelmed by a tidal wave of negative self-talk and low self-worth. I perpetually felt not good enough, not good, not enough, just … not.

Bittman's mantra told me that "good enough" was, indeed, "good enough." Another popular take on this is the saying, "The perfect is the enemy of the good." This idea is what got me through my dissertation. My friends and I would routinely ask each other, "Do you want to write an award-winning dissertation, or do you want to finish?"—the implication being that the obsession with perfection and being "award-winning" would paralyze you from actually completing the work. And I do know people who never finished their dissertations, so this was not just a cute motivational saying but an actual possibility. Also, one of my friends *did* finish *and* write an award-winning dissertation, so the two are not mutually exclusive.

Similar in philosophy to Bittman, I had a highly celebrated professor in graduate school (Dr. William Schubert) who scaled his syllabus to earn a B average in his class. What this meant was that if you did all the outlined work and showed up for class, you would earn a B. However, if you felt "compelled" or were "so obsessed with

> Coming to terms with being average or "good enough" gave me the freedom to stop my self-flagellation and constant inner critic. It gave me room to consider what was important to me and where I would put my energy... [and] absolution for making choices that others might make differently.

your grade that you had to have an A" (his words), you wrote an extra paper in addition to the regular classwork. In other words, if you did everything that was expected, you received a B, and that was a perfectly acceptable thing. Of course, the first course I took with Schubert, I *had* to write the extra paper and get the A. By the time I took two other courses with him, later in my graduate coursework, I willingly took the B. I realized that I had to make decisions about what I could manage timewise, and that the extra paper did not necessarily mean I learned more in writing it.

Bittman's "good enough" gave me permission to shake off the heavy chains of expectations and of constantly trying to measure up to some imagined excellence. And humorously enough, it has pushed me into lots of funny spaces where I am definitely above- average and may possibly even excel. I am an ultra-runner, which means I run distances longer than a marathon (26.2 miles). After running more than a dozen marathons at a slightly above average pace (and a couple at definitely above average), I wanted to try something different and turned towards ultra-marathons. And ultra-marathoners are a funny group. They pride

themselves on being back-of-the-packers (i.e., dead last or close to it), because they know what they're doing is totally nuts and beyond the realm of understanding for most people. So even if they're *below* average as ultra-runners, they know they are doing something extra-ordinary. As an ultra-runner, I also won my first age-group race. True, I think there were only six other runners in that category, but I still won. After years of running races and having my kids ask me if I won, I could finally say yes.

It was running that also made me realize what I valued and the importance of balancing what you love and what you do. Because I was trained as a researcher at a research-intensive (R1) university, I was taught to believe that publishing was your value as an academic. Being a good teacher was fine, but publishing was more important. Even though this was not the culture at Lewis University, I believed my value was premised on my productivity as a scholar. All my academic friends were at R1 universities, and I found myself caught up in writing support groups and accountability check-ins. It was through these check-ins and seeing friends talk about getting up at five a.m. to write before their workday that I had an epiphany. I would willingly, sometimes joyfully, get up at five a.m. to run twenty miles and put my body through the wringer. However, I found no joy and little willingness to do this with my writing most of the time, so I gave myself permission to stop trying to do something in a way that didn't work for me. I put my running ahead of my writing, and I found joy.

Ironically, I also found a willingness to write, but mostly in community with others. I wasn't worried about publishing only in top-tier journals or being the sole author on an article (something prized at R1 universities). While those things were nice, they were not the things I privileged over my sleep or my family or my running. Instead, I found myself writing books about the things I enjoyed or found important, and I wrote with friends instead of writing alone. I have realized that being in community with others, intellectually, spiritually, in friendship, was of the highest priority. I just finished writing my third collaborative book and have ideas for two more. A friend recently commented on my CV (a Curriculum Vitae is an exhaustively longer version of a résumé) and the unconventional nature of it (for education)—three books but relatively few peer-reviewed articles. I shrugged but also reveled in the choices I have made. Being tied to someone else's idea of excellence would have found me tearing out my hair alone while pounding away at my keyboard in the wee hours of the morning, muttering about poor life choices.

Speaking of CVs, I think some people would find the breadth of my scholarship a bit puzzling. I wrote my dissertation on hip-hop in the classroom, my first two books are about teaching with graphic novels, and my current book is about Asian American teachers' racialization. In graduate school, I struggled with having so many different areas of interest. Those who finished their doctorate most quickly were those who were single-mindedly driven on their specific topic, and all their reading and writing were in service of understanding their topic. I read too many different things and attended too many different conferences, but I also found this stimulating. I enjoy being curious and reading and writing on a variety of topics. While this is less "productive" in the traditional academic sense of the word, I find it feeds me in a way that single-minded productivity would not.

I also ended up running for school board—with a friend of course—because I figured I was no worse than the others that had run or were running for office, and I might even have something to offer that some of the other candidates didn't (I was the only one that was running that had an education background). And I did consider that my face (being Asian) and my name (the same as the leader of North Korea) might be barriers for some votes, but I wouldn't know if I didn't at least try. Being freed from the "all or nothing" pattern of thought, the "If I don't win, I'm a loser," gave me the courage to try something that scared me. The worst thing that could happen was that I would lose, and many others had lost and survived. Not only did I win, I won by the most votes, and I was voted in as the Vice-President, now President, of the school board.

Freedom to Grow

Coming to terms with being average or "good enough" gave me the freedom to stop my self-flagellation and constant inner critic. It gave me room to consider what was important to me and where I would put my energy. It also gave me absolution for making choices that others might make differently. Some might think that the idea of embracing "good enough" implies laziness or constant mediocrity. Quite the opposite, it's allowed me to think about the ways in which I can excel in some areas and ways in which I can be below average in others.

One thing that people sometimes confuse with average is that it is not the median, meaning it is not the absolute middle number all the time. Average is the culmination evened out of both the ups and downs, the excellence and failure. By thinking about the possibilities for average, I can see the ways others shine or fall as well. So, my measure of success or happiness or completion will always be different from another's. There is no universal success

or failure. This can be a hard thing to remember sometimes, when I see some friends getting an endless number of awards or churning out publications. If that is my only measure of success, then I am failing. Let me tell you, though, I love teaching and having relationships with my students. I am more committed to their lifelong learning— and those of their own students—than I am to writing an article ten people might read. I won't say I am the absolute best teacher, but I think my students would definitely say I'm above average. Maybe some days I am the best teacher, and other days I am tired. However, I made the choice to prioritize being fully in that classroom and making those connections.

I have a silly comic I bought as a print (@dinocomics). Two dinosaurs are talking, and one says, "Oh I failed." The other dinosaur says, "As long as you tried your best, you didn't fail." To which, the first dinosaur replies, "Oh I didn't do that either." I bought this print as a tongue-in-cheek reminder that we can't always give our all or expect others to constantly give their all, and that it's ok. And that maybe we can even laugh about it. If my current vocation is about embracing and accepting being "good enough," and even preaching that particular gospel, I'd be pretty happy about it.

Looking Beyond the Numbers

by Joseph Kozminski, Ph.D.

Professor and Chair, Department of Physics

It was a crisp October morning. Several holes into a mediocre round of golf in what would be my last high school tournament, I came up to the tee box on a 180-yard par 3. The pin was back, behind a ridge, so that I couldn't see the cup. I hit a good shot toward the pin but didn't catch all of it. When we walked up to the green, my ball wasn't there. I, and everyone in my group, assumed my ball hit the back of the ridge and shot off the green. After searching amidst the leaves and black walnuts on the ground, the coach monitoring our group asked if I had checked the hole. There it was—a hole-in-one! That shot energized me and turned my round around. I ended up finishing in the top twenty in the region, a couple of strokes from making state, an unlikely end to a high school career that could easily have never gotten off the ground.

Looking back after that round, I felt incredibly fortunate and grateful to have made it that far. Four years earlier when I was trying out for the team, I was the quiet, anxious, nerdy kid with the mismatched golf clubs and unorthodox swing. I had never had lessons; I learned the game from my dad and grandpa. I had a decent short game and played strategically, but I wasn't a long-hitter, and tee to green could be an adventure. If I plotted my scores that summer going into tryouts (okay, I did that), it would look like an EKG readout. I could compete as easily as I could shoot a big number. Going into the last day of tryouts, I was hanging right around the cut line. My game that day, like my season, was erratic. Talking to the others afterwards, I calculated that my score didn't make the cut. However, when I was finally called into the clubhouse, unexpected news awaited. Coach Cherrette said that he saw potential in me and that I was going to get the last spot on the team as his "project" if I was willing to put in the work. While the rest of the team was out on the course during practices, I was on the practice range with Coach where he rebuilt my swing during the first several weeks of the season. It was frustrating; I wanted to be out there with my teammates instead of hitting ball after ball on the range. In time, I was allowed to go out and finish the last few holes with the team, and by the end of the season, play some full practice rounds.

For the rest of my high school golf career, I had to continue to work at it. In sophomore and even junior year, I sometimes slipped back into old habits and missed cuts to play in matches the following week. I worked through these slumps, and Coach never gave up on me. Instead, he gave me more responsibility, having me work with some of the younger players during practice, and sometimes, after practice, he would pull me aside and mentor me on team leadership. Looking back, I think he liked my coachability as well as my persistence and my even demeanor on the course, not getting too high or too low. While there were better golfers on the team, Coach named me a co-captain my senior year, again looking at more than just the numbers.

This experience taught me grit and perseverance, and certainly some humility. It wasn't easy to be the freshman "project," stuck on the driving range, and it was disheartening to miss matches during a junior year slump. It would have been easy to walk away; I sometimes wondered if I really belonged on the team anyway. However, Coach took a chance on me, and I wasn't going to squander the opportunity.

I also learned that numbers aren't everything. It would have been easy for Coach to set the cut line and take the top sixteen golfers. However, he rode around the course all week during tryouts watching us play and getting to know us. I wasn't just a number to him; I was a person with strengths and weaknesses who needed, and would respond to, some coaching and mentoring. As a teacher, I also try to look beyond the numbers, beyond the grades and the ACT scores, and give everyone a chance. The numbers are a metric, but they only tell part of the story. The person and the context are just as important, if not more important.

When thinking about the journey that led me to where I am today, it is filled with people and experiences like this one. These have helped define me and shape my values and worldview and have helped me find my vocation as an educator.

I grew up in Grand Rapids, Michigan, in a family that valued science and education. My parents sacrificed to send my brother and me to Catholic schools for grade school and high school because they wanted us to have a high-quality education. My parents were both the first in their families to attend college, and both ended up majoring in the sciences, my mother in biology (after initially going to college to become a nun) and my father in math and physics before going on for a master's in math. I have always been curious about the world and loved science and math from an early age. My childhood included nature walks, museum trips, PBS documentaries, and the occasional summer science or math camp. I loved going to the planetarium and learning about space; building my own creations with LEGOs; working in the garden with my mom, who grew up on a farm and had a wealth of knowledge to share; and collecting and identifying rocks, leaves, or whatever else I was curious about at the time. My father's first faculty position was in computer science at a local college; thus, I had access to a computer at home since early elementary school (I didn't see a computer in school until fifth grade) and learned to program a little BASIC and Logo, though my attempt at creating a computer game never panned out. But my parents also encouraged well-roundedness. I enjoyed playing sports—basketball, baseball, soccer, and, of course, golf—though I wasn't very athletic. I went to an occasional theatre performance or pops orchestra concert, and I played trumpet through high school. I came to value STEAM (Science, Technology, Engineering, Arts, and Mathematics) well before that acronym existed.

As an introvert, I also relished escaping into a good book, and I read widely and voraciously. Fortunately, I had ready access to books. My mom, a part-time medical technologist, volunteered at my school's library for as long as I can remember. She took on more and more responsibility, becoming head volunteer and then eventually getting hired as a school librarian and media center coordinator. My mom would regularly bring home boxes of books to process, and I would gladly help since it was an opportunity to find new reads before they hit the library shelves. I still always have at least one book going that is not related to my work. Sometimes, I read to de-stress and jump into another world; other times, I read

to expand my worldview, to see things from a new perspective, and to learn.

So, when did I consider education as a career path? In a way, as the product of two educators, it had always been in my mind. I always loved to learn, and over time, especially when I started tutoring in high school, I discovered that when I helped others learn, I was able to understand the material better myself. When I got to the University of Notre Dame, I jumped at the opportunity to be a tutor for the introductory physics sequence for majors as soon as I was eligible in my second year and held this role for my remaining years there. It was challenging, especially early on when I was still wrestling with the material myself, but when something would click for a student, I felt like I was making a difference. I knew that wherever I landed later, I wanted to have an opportunity to teach.

Also, during my high school and college years, I really recognized the importance of reflection. Those years were full of activity and growth, and I needed time to take a step back and process things, to piece together what was happening in school, in my life, and in the world around me. Whether gardening, going for a hike or a bike ride, or walking down the fairway, I have found nature to be an especially great place of escape, peace, and inspiration, and a good place to reflect, think, and de-stress. Engaging in reflection provides an opportunity to process what went well and what I could do better next time and to mentally prepare for upcoming activities. Reflection has allowed

> **"**
> I wasn't just a number to him; I was a person with strengths and weaknesses who needed, and would respond to, some coaching and mentoring.
> **"**

me to continue growing and improving as a teacher, researcher, and mentor.

I had other opportunities at Notre Dame that solidified my passion for teaching as well. In my second year, I tried to get involved in research, but most research groups I talked to were unwilling to take on a second-year student who had only finished the introductory physics sequence and wasn't at the top of the class. However, Drs. Mitch Wayne and Randy Ruchti in the high energy physics group gave me a chance. During my five semesters with the group, they put me on projects that sounded daunting. My classes didn't teach me anything about testing the properties of scintillating fibers for particle tracking detectors or about designing electro-optical readout boxes. However, my research advisors provided a great support structure and mentoring to get me up to speed, and I was eager to learn and contribute to the projects.

During this time, Randy also engaged me in outreach through the QuarkNet group, which he had co-founded a couple years earlier to bring high energy physics to high school teachers and students. Suddenly, I found myself with an informal teaching experience out in the community,

engaging with kids and their families at various outreach events. Little did I know that in the spring of my junior year, this would lead to Randy taking me to a Congressional Science Fair at the Rayburn House Building in Washington, D.C., to showcase a portable cosmic ray detector the group had developed for outreach (Baumbaugh).

Now, this was a big day for me. First, I had never been on an airplane or on any public transit other than a bus, let alone four airplanes and the Metro in one day. My parents didn't really enjoy traveling, and my mom never flew in her life. We typically took an annual driving vacation, alternating between Northern Michigan/the Upper Peninsula and Chicago, though we did do a couple of longer road trips, including D.C., the summer before my little brother was born. I, on the other hand, had always wanted to fly and to explore the country, and I was thrilled to bring our science outreach to House members and staff. On the flight, Randy reviewed the detector and the physics and gave me a crash course on engaging in outreach with government officials. Aside from the organizer, Rep. Vern Ehlers, a Ph.D. physicist, most of the people we talked to did not have a background in science, so in some ways it was like doing a community outreach event.

House members mostly sent staff to the event, though I did get to meet a few House members themselves. One interaction that day stood out. An aide for a longtime House member came up to me and asked where we got the camera we were using to display the images from the detector on a monitor. I was not expecting this question. This wasn't what we went to Washington to present; it was just a digital camera from a big box electronics store. The aide was totally missing the point! However, I took Randy's coaching from the plane and ran with the question. I snuck in some information about the detector and the particle tracks streaking across the screen, but I felt that I didn't do my job of presenting the project very well since the big takeaway for the aide seemed to be the digital camera, not our project or the science.

This experience taught me several important things. The first was how important it is for scientists to engage with and educate government officials and policy makers. Most are not scientists, but they make policy and funding decisions that affect science. The second was about finding some common ground for engagement; for that aide, it was the camera. This opened the door for a conversation, regardless of how ineffectively I thought I presented our work. The third lesson took me years of returning to that interaction to sink in. We were not there just to showcase our work, but we were there as advocates and ambassadors for science in general. Studies have shown that only about forty percent of the American public have a great deal of confidence in leaders in the scientific community (Arvizu), and fewer than twenty percent can name a living scientist (Benson). Therefore, if the aide walked away having had a positive interaction with me and I was able to start breaking down a potential barrier or bias, that was a win.

While I had many good experiences like these as an undergraduate, I was also awakened to some issues in the field that needed to be addressed. In the introductory physics sequence for majors, we started with fifty students in the class. The professor droned on for two, two-hour lectures each week, writing feverishly on the board with little interaction with the class, and gave quizzes and tests on which thirty percent of the questions were a "learning experience." It was brutal! If the primary objective was weeding students out, it did its job. Students were withdrawing left and right, and by the start of the second semester, we were down to about twenty students. By the start of the third semester, we were down to twelve, and by the end of that semester, the only woman still in the group changed her major to electrical engineering.

At the time, I didn't know anything about high-impact, active learning strategies or physics education research (which was being conducted at only a handful of places with few studies yet on equitable and inclusive classroom environments in physics) or about the lack of diversity in physics in general, but this "weeding out" of students just didn't seem right. Looking back, it is clear that this classroom exemplified the systemic inequities that led to so few women and students of color majoring in physics, and even fewer going on for Ph.Ds. Those who dropped out of physics were smart people who could have made it but went on to find success in engineering, medicine, business, and other endeavors instead. I made it through the gauntlet of chemistry, calculus, and physics in my first year, but I knew that there had to be a better approach to teaching than what I had experienced, and this stuck with me.

When I started graduate school, I was a teaching assistant with my own sections of a general education astronomy lab. Having received minimal pedagogy training before being turned loose, however, I modeled my teaching on some of the excellent instructors I had had as an undergrad and experimented to see what kinds of engagement seemed effective. I didn't have a lot of latitude since these were prescribed, cookbook-like, simulation-based labs, but I was able to establish a good rapport with the students. Most made it through, and my evaluations were good, so that was an initial success.

When I went to Fermilab to do research for my dissertation, I no longer had the opportunity to teach, and the longer I was there, the more I missed teaching. I got involved in outreach with the Fermilab Education Office, and I picked up some side work tutoring high school students in

math and physics. It was around this time that I also joined the American Association of Physics Teachers (AAPT) and started attending Chicago Section (CSAAPT) meetings. I also started digging into physics education research articles and learning about effective teaching practices. I knew that teaching was my calling and that applying for faculty positions at smaller colleges instead of doing postdocs and vying for a position at a large research university was the path for me. Fortunately, my advisor, Dr. Harry Weerts, was very supportive, and he even let me pick up an adjunct position teaching Astronomy of the Solar System at a community college during my final semester of graduate school.

At the community college, I finally had my own classes, more autonomy, and, of course, new challenges. The students were very diverse, reflecting a wide range of demographics and experiences. Many students were first-generation college students, and most were working while going to school. One section included more traditional-aged students and the other split between traditional-aged students and working adults. I learned quickly that what worked in one section didn't always work as well in the other section, and what worked for some students didn't always work for others. I tried to make things relevant and engaging, like I would at an outreach event, and I tried to apply some of the physics education research I had read about and had heard about at CSAAPT meetings. Some things worked; some things flopped. However, I again was able to build a good rapport with the classes and got to know the students, which went a long way when things didn't work or when I made a mistake, and as an inexperienced teacher, there were certainly plenty of those.

During my sixteen years at Lewis, I have been able to apply what I have learned from all these experiences, and I have continued to grow through new experiences and professional development opportunities. I have found mentors at Lewis and in the wider physics community, especially through CSAAPT and AAPT, and continue to learn from them. I have said "yes" to a range of professional and service opportunities that have come my way. I have even made a foray into politics, being elected to the Board of Education of my local public school district, since I believe scientists need to be more active and engaged in advocacy, government, and policymaking. These activities all tie into improving education and having a positive impact on students.

Whether I am in the classroom, mentoring students in research, at an outreach event in the community, or advocating for science and education, I am trying to make a connection and to educate. As an educator and a scientist, I continue to reflect, to experiment, to learn—not only about physics and physics education, but also about the world around me—and to improve.

Former United Nations Secretary-General Kofi Annan noted, "Education is a human right with immense power to transform. On its foundation rest the cornerstones of freedom, democracy, and sustainable human development" (Annan 4). All students deserve a high-quality education and a chance to succeed, and I hope to provide this. Just like my high school golf coach looked beyond the scorecard and gave me a chance, I give every student in my classes a chance and try to ensure that the necessary supports are there if they need them. As a professor and department chair, my students' successes are the holes-in-one that energize me and keep pushing me forward.

Works Cited

Annan, Kofi A. Forward. *The State of the World's Children 1999: Education*, by Carol Bellamy, UNICEF/United Nations Children's Fund, 1999, p. 4. https://www.unicef.org/media/84771/file/SOWC-1999.pdf

Arvizu, Dan E., et al. "Science & Engineering Indicators 2016." *National Science Board*, 2016. https://www.nsf.gov/statistics/2016/nsb20161/uploads/1/nsb20161.pdf

Baumbaugh, B., et al. "A Portable Cosmic Ray Detector and Display." *1999 IEEE Nuclear Science Symposium. Conference Record. 1999 Nuclear Science Symposium and Medical Imaging Conference* (Cat. No.99CH37019), 1999, pp. 783-785, vol. 2, doi: 10.1109/NSSMIC.1999.845784.

Benson, H. "Can You Name a Living Scientist?" *New Voices for Research*, 2019. http://newvoicesforresearch.blogspot.com/2009/07/can-you-name-living- scientist.html

All Roads Lead the Journey

by Michele Riley Kramer, Ph.D., M.S.N., R.N., A.H.N.-B.C.

Professor, Graduate Nursing Program
Track Leader, MSN Healthcare Systems Leadership

Does one choose a vocation, or does it choose us? Everything connects to our life, each choice or decision, leading to a set of circumstances until the next decision or choice. It has taken most of my lifetime to figure out there is a difference between vocation and career, between a calling or purpose and a job, to figure out why I am here. I traversed many paths, and meandered, wondering if I was, in fact, aimlessly wandering, just following life into the next phase. I also wondered why I didn't seem to fit in with the norm of a career path because I could not seem to settle into anything that felt right for a future, or felt right for long, until only recently. What I've discovered is that all roads chosen, or chosen for us, frame the journey that our soul makes in this lifetime, that *all* roads lead the journey. I've also discovered that one's vocation can be supported using intuition and identifying the synchronicities that direct the journey.

Context and Background

The world was a bewildering place growing up. Part of my journey included a nomadic existence during the first half of my life. Being in a military family, we moved frequently, never living more than three years in one place. At one point as an adolescent, we moved five times in three years, moving from Virginia to a small town in Germany, then to a city in Germany, on to a town in northern Italy, and then to a town in Oklahoma. Until that last move, the transitions nearly always occurred in the middle of the school year. I said goodbye to old friends and learned to make new friends; I adapted to new cities, towns, countries—catching up, or being ahead of what was currently being taught in the new school. I would start to settle in and then move again. At the time, I often felt scared and alone. Looking back, I see there were also positives. I learned to adapt to new situations and environments, developing a process for settling into each new place.

I learned that change is an inevitable part of life. I became skilled at talking to people and learning about them. I viewed each encounter as an exercise in curiosity and getting people to talk about themselves—which now contributes significantly to my skill as a nurse and educator. One of my faculty colleagues often remarks how I can go into a room full of different faculty and find someone to talk to—in fact, that I seek out others not in my college.

I have always been curious. Curiosity fuels my growth and learning and keeps life, well, lively! My favorite means of learning are dialoging ideas, listening to formal presentations, and reading books. Books especially have a special significance in my life. I would often come across books addressing whatever I was interested in at the time, as if they magically fell into my lap! It still happens to this day. For instance, I teach a class about the dynamics of healthcare organizations. After reading a great deal on how organizations operate today, I began to wonder whether organizations are evolving and how they would look. One day, an email newsletter appeared that led me to intuitively discover a book by Frederic Laloux called *Reinventing Organizations*. It explains the next evolution of organizations and opened a new avenue for thought-provoking discussion with my students, introducing them to a new view of organizations they were unlikely to encounter elsewhere.

I thought these magical experiences happened that way only with me until I was conducting research for my dissertation study. My research population was long-term practitioners of Integral Yoga, a system of accessing the Divine put forth by a 20th century sage from India named Sri Aurobindo. As part of my data collection, I asked each participant how they came to practice Integral Yoga. A majority said they came across a book by Sri Aurobindo that resonated with them at a time they were seeking a spiritual direction. A couple of participants described walking by a bookstore they passed by often and intuitively getting the urge to go inside where they found the book they were seeking but didn't know it.

Similarly, synchronistic events occur frequently for me. A synchronicity, according to depth psychologist Carl Jung, is a meaningful coincidence—when two or more things occur together that have no apparent connection to each other but seemingly connect. We may not understand the connections until years later. Synchronicities abound in life if we pay attention to them.

Career and Vocation

Synchronicities and intuitive guidance occurred throughout my life and career.

How I became a nurse and educator involved a convoluted journey where one choice didn't seem to connect to the next in a meaningful way until I was able to look back on it. During my late teenage rebellion, which often occurs between mother and daughter, my mother, who trained as a nurse, informed me during a heated argument one day that I was too cold-hearted to be a nurse. I decided to prove her wrong, which started me on my career path, although I did not know it at the time. To attend nursing school, I knew I would have to pay for college or take out hefty loans. Someone mentioned that the Air Force had a nursing scholarship that paid full tuition for four years. I went down to the recruiting office, which also housed recruiting offices from other military branches. The Air Force recruiter wasn't there that day, but the Army recruiter was and informed me that the Army, not the Air Force, had the full-ride scholarship. I took the information but didn't immediately do anything with it as I wasn't sure how it would fit with my plans for going to school with my boyfriend. The week before the deadline for applying for the scholarship, my boyfriend broke up with me. That fueled my decision to apply, and I somehow got the application in by the deadline. I won the scholarship, an elite one. The uniqueness of that nursing program, its cutting-edge education, opened me to new ideas regarding nursing and untapped human capacities. The synchronicity of these events—the argument with my mother, the break-up with my boyfriend, and the absence of the Air Force recruiter—seemingly unconnected, started my career path and eventual vocation.

At the time, I can't say that I embraced nursing as my career choice. I felt as if I were led to it because I got into an elite nursing program that also kept me in the military environment I'd grown up in, which was comforting. And nursing was a stable career. In my first nursing role in the emergency room, I encountered situations where I was helpless to make someone's condition better, or at least bearable, a feeling I did not like. Often these situations involved someone in deep pain where the physician was unable or unwilling to prescribe anything to alleviate the pain, or there was no treatment to relieve it. If someone was dying, I didn't know how to ease their journey or instill hope.

During that time—another synchronicity—as I was in a relationship with a psychotherapist who knew about transpersonal psychology and the human potential movement, an emerging force in psychology at the time. This movement proposed that human beings had capacities beyond what science already knew, that humans had a spiritual force within and the capacity to heal themselves beyond Western medical knowledge. Transpersonal psychology, as part of the human potential movement, explored spirituality and consciousness beyond our waking awareness—the intangibles connected to human existence. The movement introduced the West to Eastern spiritual wisdom, traditions, ideas, and practices, thousands of years old, that integrated the mind-body-spirit, reflecting a cohesive, whole human being. The movement's proponents were based in Northern California, where I was living at the time. They validated my intuitive belief that there was more to the

> **"**
>
> A synchronicity...is a meaningful coincidence—when two or more things occur together that have no apparent connection to each other but seemingly connect. We may not understand the connections until years later. Synchronicities abound in life if we pay attention to them.
>
> **"**

human condition than what I experienced and understood so far and offered an answer to the helplessness I was experiencing as a nurse. I sought out as many opportunities to learn and incorporate what I learned into my nursing practice, walking both sides of this fence—traditional and alternative—for the rest of my career.

Despite discovering an alternative approach to nursing, I've often tried to leave nursing. What helped me stay was discovering nursing theorist Martha Rogers' definition that nursing was about people and their world. Rogers' theory, the Science of Unitary Human Beings, proposes that each of us are energy fields interacting with other energy fields and the environment in ever-increasing complexity and diversity, a theory that was congruent with my knowledge of alternative health and holistic nursing. From her description, I could now see how nursing embodied all that I knew and learned about caring for human beings.

I worked in a variety of settings and roles: emergency room and medical-surgical nurse; nurse practitioner working in internal medicine oncology and women's healthcare settings; hospital staff development/educator; legislative aide; and nursing

licensure exam test developer. I could not settle into any specialization. Finally, during another move that necessitated finding a new job, I took a job in nursing education at a small community hospital and discovered that I loved to teach. Teaching was creative, dynamic, and fed my curiosity. I loved imparting new knowledge to others. I did not see teaching as a calling, however, until years later.

I want to share a story that represents another synchronicity that connects me to my calling. A lot of effort and stress are involved in getting an advanced degree. I vowed after I got my masters' degree that if I ever got a doctoral degree, it would be in something I loved, something that passionately interested me. At some point, I realized I wanted to teach at the graduate level and somehow incorporate my years of experience and learning in holistic health. I also needed an accredited program to make my degree legitimate for most academic settings. Such programs are difficult to find. About a month before the application due date (this will seem familiar to you), I ran across a small advertisement in a journal I hadn't subscribed to but showed up in my mail. It was about an accredited university that had a Ph.D. in humanistic and transpersonal psychology with a concentration in consciousness and spirituality—exactly what I was looking for. After contacting them for more information, I put the idea aside to ponder. About a week before the application deadline, the university contacted me to remind me of the deadline, and I intuitively knew this addressed my passion—my search for my soul's purpose—and would expand my nursing knowledge about people and healing. Madly scrambling, I got everything in and was accepted. I later found out the faculty were the movers and shakers of the human potential movement that I became involved in at the beginning of my nursing career. I had come full circle.

Nursing is my career. Teaching is my vocation. Teaching graduate nursing for over eleven years, I realize that I like seeing the light bulbs go on over students' heads when they grasp a concept or make a connection, changing the way they perceive their world. I enjoy showing them another way to think, a different way to look at something, and expanding their perception of life and humanity. It's magical! Teaching is my vocation because it provides a creative vehicle to support this magic, and it feeds my soul.

Some know their purpose and vocation early in life and focus solely on pursuing it. Others, like me, do not discover it until they are farther along in their career and life's journey. Healthcare and academia expect those involved in these fields to specialize in some topic early and pursue it over the course of their careers. I could not commit to this expectation. In the introduction of his book *Range* (2019), David Epstein tells the story of two world-class athletes who took different paths in the beginning but ended at the same level of expertise. He explains how one came from a focused specialist approach, showing a clearly identifiable talent for one sport and groomed from a very early age for it (Tiger Woods). The other enjoyed and played several sports but didn't settle on one until later in his life. He took a more meandering, exploratory approach (Roger Federer). Both devoted the hours it requires to achieve mastery in their sport, but their early journeys were different. The descriptions given for these two approaches are specialist and generalist, respectively. In our current society, specialization is more valued than generalization. Being a generalist can feel uncomfortable, but the book helped me understand why I initially felt uncomfortable in my profession, as if I didn't quite fit. I have a different gift.

Gifts, Lessons, Takeaways

I am grateful for the care and protection from the Universe as I moved through my life, leading me to know my vocation and reason for being on this Earth plane. I wish to share some insights about life and calling from my journey that may guide you in understanding and forging your soul's path. These insights can be seen as a map that lights the way. Take away what feels right for you.

1. **Synchronicities abound.** They enrich life's meaning, offering important clues, understanding, and connections about your unique journey. Look for them.

2. **EVERY experience offers gifts and lessons.** Divining what they are provides clues to who you are and who you are becoming.

3. **Trust and honor your intuition.** Seek to interpret its messages. Intuition connects us to our soul—a spark of the Divine in each of us. Practice tapping into it and use it especially when you're at a crossroads.

4. **Pay attention to the intangibles in life that are not easily seen or accepted or proven (like intuition) but, nevertheless, are there.** They bring a wealth of information to be sensed, experienced, and responded to. They include such things as spirituality, love, healing, hope, gratitude, joy, and the human energy field that surrounds us.

5. **Cultivate a sense of awe and discovery.** Be flexible, open-minded, curious, adaptable, and aware of what life brings you and how life *supports* your journey. At any age, to prompt new growth, periodically ask: "What do I want to be when I grow up again?"

6. **Surround yourself with friends who support your journey and help clarify your purpose,** friends who can help you reflect on important questions like: *What am I drawn to? Does this bring me joy? Is this meaningful to me? Does this challenge or bring out the best in me?*

7. **Be all that you are.** You may not align with the expectations of your chosen professional career, and there is nothing wrong with that or you. It is okay to be a curious, life-learning "generalist" in a field that values over-specialization. Be confident in knowing that what you offer is of equal or more value.

8. **Pay attention to your thoughts and feelings.** Thoughts are energy; what we think becomes our reality. Change your thoughts when they no longer honor and support you. One of my guiding principles that evolved from living a nomadic life is: "If you can't change the situation, change the way you look at it."

9. **Finally, view your passions as clues to who you are, where you want to go, and who you want to become.** They will sustain you in your pursuits.

Our purpose in this life is to evolve to our highest degree. How we evolve, what we accomplish, and how we feel and reflect upon both becomes the journey. Life is about exploring who we are, nurturing the soul we came in with, and how to best express our soul's intention. Our calling, our vocation, is the portal for our journey.

The Phone Booth

by Brother Joseph Martin, FSC, D. Min.

Special Assistant to the President (Retired)

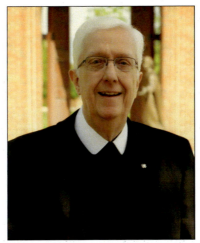

At the other end of the phone line, I heard Marie say, "Do it!" I was on the verge of making a major life decision. Those two words confirmed the direction I was headed.

It was June of 1996. Marie lived in Cincinnati, and I lived in Indianapolis. She is a religious Sister and had been my spiritual director for about seven years. We met regularly in person one hour each month. Over the years, she was exceptionally non-directive, at most suggesting that I "might" like to read this or that book or article. She was attentive to the concerns and issues that I raised. I was a campus minister at the University of Cincinnati, and I was living in a local parish rectory, thus outside a Brothers' community. The Franciscan Friars administered the parish, so I still had some elements of religious life with them, and I made regular visits back to the Brothers for retreats and jubilees. I served on the Board of Trustees of the Brothers' college and on their Provincial Council. So, while I lived separate from them, I was not isolated.

A native Detroiter, I had joined the Brothers right out of high school given the inspiration of two men at Austin Catholic Prep sponsored by the Chicago Province of the Augustinians. One was Thomas Bailey who taught English and French and who made learning an enjoyable experience. We had fun in his class, and we learned a lot. He had a well-deserved reputation as a top-notch teacher among other Catholic high schools around Detroit. He inspired me to be a teacher because of his sense of humor and his focus on our education. Something inside me clicked with the thought of being a teacher, especially because during high school I was tutoring grade school students in my neighborhood with their math homework. That was the first indication that I wanted to work with people. I did not know if I could be a teacher, but I had to try it to find out.

The other person was Brother Chris McCartney, an Augustinian Brother who was Assistant Disciplinarian at the school. He was not a teacher, but he always mingled with the students at dances, proms, football and basketball games, and the annual Friar Festival which raised money for the school. He was a young man, and his friendliness, genuine interest in students, and pleasant personality attracted me to the notion of being a Brother. I had no idea what the life of a Brother was like, but I was inspired to learn if community life was for me. Like many other Brothers have reported, I joined because I wanted to teach, and eventually I grew into community life. But since Augustinian Brothers could not teach, I looked elsewhere. With the advantage of hindsight, I see that God was calling me through those two men.

At home, our family subscribed to *Sign Magazine*, a national Catholic publication of the Passionist Fathers. Besides feature articles, it contained display ads for priests and for congregations for Sisters and Brothers. I looked through them for Brothers who were teachers. I picked five and mailed letters to them requesting details about their lives and ministries. When I received responses, I pitched two immediately which were impersonal, mimeographed form letters. Of the others, the Brothers of the Poor of St. Francis in Cincinnati told me that I did not have a calling to their order, mainly because they only conducted orphanages. I discarded the response from the De La Salle Christian Brothers because I did not like their black robe and could not see myself wearing it. That left me with the order I chose. I prefer not to name this group, so I will call them the Education Brothers. After several letters

and a visit with the Vocation Director, I decided to join them and entered the novitiate in the fall of 1963, with the support of my parents and friends. Everything was proceeding well, and I enjoyed living with the Brothers, so I pronounced my first vows in 1964 and my final vows in 1969. I taught in their New York state boarding school from 1967 to 1980, where I learned that I enjoyed teaching and modeled my classes after Tom Bailey.

Like other religious congregations, the Education Brothers were facing the changes in the church and in society and the consequent diminishment in the number of all Brothers, Sisters, and priests. Our Province was especially impacted: With regular deaths of the older men, we were reduced to about fifty Education Brothers in the U.S. Our headquarters were in a small New England town, and we were limited to four educational ministries. That did not provide significant opportunities for Brothers to serve in teaching or administration. After teaching in high school, I accepted a position as Director of Public Relations at their only college. Two years later, I decided that being a public relations director was not for me, especially because my lay supervisor was always pointing out every minor mistake I made and rarely had a word of praise.

So, I looked outside the four ministries and found a position in campus ministry at the University of Cincinnati working with the Franciscan Friars. It was a life-giving ministry with new colleagues and opened

> **"**
> I had no idea what the life of a Brother was like, but I was inspired to learn if community life was for me. Like many other Brothers have reported, I joined because I wanted to teach, and eventually I grew into community life.
> **"**

a new world of opportunities to me. While I continued my interest in spirituality, I learned about other religions through the campus ministers of other faiths. Then Archbishop Daniel Pilarczyk appointed me to represent religious Brothers on the Archdiocesan Pastoral Council. During those years, I was also appointed to the Board of Trustees of the Education Brothers' college, and I was elected to the Brothers' Provincial Council of the U.S. District. After several years in Cincinnati, I applied for and was accepted as the Program Director at Fatima Retreat House in Indianapolis, where I could make good use of my people skills. Once again, I lived in a local parish rectory.

While all these exciting opportunities were happening, I was disappointed and dismayed. As our older Brothers died, we had no new men joining us. The lack of ministries in the District meant that I would need to seek outside positions. I had tried many times to encourage the Education Brothers to try new prayer forms, new ministries, and to adapt our community life to be more genuine and appealing. Then our Brother Vocation Director decided to leave the order. If that was not bad enough,

our Provincial announced at the May 1996 Provincial Council meeting that he would not appoint a new Vocation Director because "religious life is dying, and our District is so small that we cannot hope to increase our membership." I was devastated. At age fifty-two, I had too much life and energy to give to a dying institution.

Since 1989, I had been meeting with Marie and discussing my hopes and frustrations. As noted, she was always encouraging and very much an active listener, reflecting back to me what I was saying and never telling me what to do. She respected my life and my decision-making process, and she encouraged my own searching for answers to my questions. Following the Council meeting in June 1996, I decided to drive from Indianapolis to Cincinnati to visit her without having made an appointment. It was a Saturday, and I suspected that she would not be busy. In the days before cell phones, I stopped at a phone booth when I arrived in Cincinnati. I called and asked if I could stop over to talk with her. To my great surprise, she was expecting her first directee of the day in ten minutes, and she had a full day of spiritual direction. She asked what I wanted to talk about, and I answered with words that I had never spoken out loud before because I had not yet told anyone about my discernment. I said, "I think I should transfer to another group of Brothers." Without a second of hesitation, she said, "Do it!" Marie had been very non-directive with me for all those years, so her clear and direct statement was a surprise. And standing alone in that phone booth, I thought, "If this is not God speaking to me through Marie, I have never heard God in my life." That incident changed my life.

A few days later, I scheduled an appointment with her, and we had a good conversation about the possibility of my changing to another order of Brothers. From the outset, I determined that I would look for another order of teachers in a community of Brothers only, not mixed priests and Brothers, and preferably a group in the Midwest. I headed to the library and picked up a copy of *A Guide to Religious Ministries for Catholic Men and Women*. I was looking for a group whose ministries matched my experiences: high school, college, retreats, and publishing. I had written and published several articles and edited a quarterly newsletter both for the Education Brothers and for the retreat center. Of the four Brothers' congregations I picked, the Midwest District of the De La Salle Christian Brothers looked most promising, with over twenty high schools, three universities, three retreat centers, and a publishing company. These ministries offered opportunities to use my skills and to serve other people. This was my second calling.

In July 1996, I wrote to the Vocation Director of the De La Salle Christian Brothers, and in October, I traveled to Chicago to meet with him and with the Brother Visitor, who is responsible for the De La Salle Christian Brothers in the district. In the intervening months, we kept in touch by letters and phone calls. During this time, I had been doing my homework. In Indianapolis, I spoke with a Jesuit priest and a Josephite Sister about their successful transfers to other orders. I called Marist Brother Sean Sammon and Trinitarian Brother Loughlan Sofield. Both are authors, licensed psychologists, and public speakers whom I had known and respected for years, and both were supportive of my decision and confirmed the direction I was headed. Franciscan Father Richard Rohr and Vincentian Father David Nygren had both written of the importance of men religious living in their own communities and not out on their own. They had both moved back into their respective community residences, and I was interested in living in a Brothers' community again.

I spent phone time with friends and family to seek their feedback. Interestingly, my cousin Katie spoke from her own experience when she said, "Oh, it sounds like you are going through a divorce!" Ouch!! She spoke the truth. I was breaking formal ties with the Education Brothers and then planning to commit myself to the De La Salle Christian Brothers.

After a lengthy discussion with my Provincial, I sent a letter to the Brother Visitor in November 1996 requesting to make the transfer. According to Canon Law, I would be in transition for three years living and serving with the De La Salle Christian Brothers while retaining my vowed connection with the Education Brothers. The Superiors General of both congregations gave their approval for my transfer, and in the summer of 1997, I moved to St. Mary's University in Winona, Minnesota, where I became Executive Assistant to the President.

My three transition years were an appropriate initiation to my new family, and I professed my final vows as a Christian Brother in July 2000 at Lewis University. Many family members and friends attended to support me. To this day, I believe that God was calling me to transfer, and the love and support of many others made the transition a smooth experience. Once I made the change, I never looked back because my ministry was rewarding, and I felt a strong sense of acceptance and belonging with the De La Salle Christian Brothers. Transferring was the best thing I have ever done for myself. And it all started with those two words of enthusiastic support I heard in a telephone booth on a sunny summer day. "Do it!"

That Book, This Vocation

by Pramod Mishra, Ph.D.

Professor, Department of English Studies

Part I: Fail

I failed third grade. On the day my third-grade results were to be announced, pupils, parents, and teachers all gathered on school grounds. The Headmaster, Sant Lal, read out the names. My name was never called. I went home sobbing. Mai—my mother—saw me, and said, "Bad luck has pursued me even here in Nepal. Now, even the masters have become my son's enemies." Mai was referring to her life in India, from where we had fled to exile in Nepal because my parents transgressed caste and kinship boundaries when they became husband and wife.

When the new academic year began, my classmates went to fourth grade, but I was held back. When Father returned from his travels, he said, "Sant Lal is a rascal. He failed my son for no reason," and confronted him at the school: "Why would everyone's son pass and only my son fail?" Showing the exam books to my father, Sant Lal said, "Please take a look. How can we pass him?"

He then turned to Mr. Dulal, his newly hired associate, and said, "How can anyone pass the boy with so little writing?" Father came home and told everything to Mai. The entire blue book had almost nothing in it. Only my crow-legged handwriting gave it away as mine.

My schooling had begun at age four on the auspicious day of worship to the Goddess of Learning held one spring. I had placed my slate, writing clay, and *Manohar Pothi* (*The Book of Delights*) at her feet and prayed for her blessings. And in third grade, the Goddess of Learning had bamboozled me. Every morning in school, we prayed in Sanskrit to give voice to the deaf and help the lame cross mountains. I thought they were praying about me.

Schooling had just begun in the area in the hinterlands of eastern Nepal, with a one-room schoolhouse made of bamboo twigs as walls and thatch as roof. Before that, schooling was banned by Nepal's autocratic Rana rulers. Until then, only three or four villagers in our area could read the land and contract deeds called shresta. I don't know where our first Village Chief had learned the rudiments of reading and writing or where Deputy Chief had taught himself his signature, but I grew up hearing tales about my father running away from home to Banaras, the ancient seat of learning in India, and working as a cook for two Bengali railway staff to earn his way through priestly education. But Father's scripture-explicating days were over by the time I began school. The loose leaves of the scripture had lain on the beam under the roof, gathering dust. Accidentally discovering them one day in my explorations, I had lifted a leaf only to see it crumble into pieces. I had left the sheaf alone and never asked Father about the decaying leaves.

Only a year or two before, organized schooling had begun in the village bazaar, with three desks and benches in a thatch and bamboo hut. At each desk sat one class of teenage pupils who had just begun learning the alphabet and basic arithmetic. One day when I went to school, teachers and pupils were busy smoking out a cobra that had slithered into the school. The school caught fire and in no time turned to ashes. The school then moved a mile south to an isolated public land. The boys went from yard to yard in the villages around, collecting thatch for roofing. Our three-room schoolhouse rose into shape. From the newly cleared forest came the wood for desks and benches. And from a nearby bamboo grove came the green sticks for flogging.

Pupils placed in higher grades had just begun learning the alphabet, basic arithmetic, and pahara (memorization of multiplication tables from 2 by 2 to 20 by 20). Our Village Chief had coaxed a retail grain trader named Poddar, and a sweetshop vendor, Chandra, to be our teachers. We called Chandra "Mr. Sukna" because he was skin-and-bone thin; we called Poddar "Mr. Thutliwal" because his jaws were long. Both had ventured into the Nepali hinterland from neighboring India. Both were fierce pupil beaters. Memorizing the multiplication table must have been the hardest for the ripened boys, calling for endless supplies of bamboo sticks. The boy who was to be whipped had to cut and slice his own stick and offer it to Mr. Sukna or Mr. Thutliwal.

The grocer's son, Hari, seldom memorized anything. He often played truant from school and ignored his teachers' warnings. Mr. Sukna turned him into a "chicken" every so often. To be a "chicken," a boy had to sit on his heels, push each hand around the inside of each leg, and grab each ear. The sooner the hand slipped its grip on the ear, the quicker the stick whipped out welts on the boy's thighs. The Rajbanshi boys from east of the bazaar, strong and stubborn that they were, got the stick almost every day. Seeing these much older boys turning into fowls made letters and numbers frightening things for me.

Bauwelal, a tutor from India whom Father had brought to tutor pupils in our village, fled back to India after a bout with malaria. After Bauwelal left, I hung around most days at wealthy Dauniya's Big Yard and fields with his son. Mother soon took over Bauwelal's duties while husking rice at the courtyard mortar and pestle. "Now, write ka, kha, ga, gha," was Mai's orders about the Devnagari alphabet, while she paddled the pestle with her foot. "Your days of truancy are over!

My eyes looked on the slate, but my mind saw the dancing stick over my head. Amidst the rhythmic beat of the pestle, its metal teeth biting the mortarful of grains, I labored to write ka, kha. "No, that's not how it's done." The beat of mortar and pestle ceased, but the drumbeat in my heart escalated. My mind saw the bamboo stick dancing over my head. "Is this how you write ka, kha, ga, gha?" There was fire in Mai's voice. After wiping the slate clean, I began again from scratch. But I could never get it right. I don't know why.

"Are you fooling me, boy? You think I don't know reading and writing?" Mai said.

What was reading and writing? Why so much beating and scolding for it? That morning, and many such mornings and evenings afterwards, the terror of her and my past, and the darkness that stared at us from the future, perhaps made my mother wish that I would become Kalidas, the mythical fool who became a scholar overnight by the blessings of a goddess after his daredevil crossing of a flooded river to light the candle at her temple. On the other hand, here I was—a dunce—Kalidas before his midnight crossing of the river. The black letters of the alphabet had become a Gordian's knot for me, an unscalable mountain.

Part II: Pass

The three-room schoolhouse stood in an isolated place, miles south from our village. My classmates and I walked from home to school and back, mornings and afternoons. In the storm season, hail the size of conch shells with horns fell from the sky, scurrying us to take shelter under the mango, the only tree around. Rabid dogs roamed the roads.

For our teacher, Mr. Sukna, memorizing the multiplication table was the be-all and end-all of education. I was good at neither the multiplication table nor handwriting. One day I forgot to bring my handwriting to school. Mr. Sukna asked for it: "Parmodhwa! Did you forget to eat your yoghurt and rice today? Hi hi hi hi!!!" Sukna's thin frame seemed to collapse with glee. Whenever I heard my distorted name, I smelled trouble. He turned to the class, "Look at him! Ahead of everyone in gluttony; behind everyone in diligence. He came to school today without breaking his yoghurt pot."

He then ordered those who hadn't brought their handwriting to climb on the desk. With much fuss and sarcasm, showing his paan-rotten, i.e., tobacco-rotten, teeth, he began to strike on the boys' legs, one by one. I became deaf to the boys' moans or groans. My skin twitched and waited for the switch to strike. And soon my calves burnt, and warm liquid flowed down my pants and soaked the desk. The boys from the bazaar and east village gave me a new name—Parmoot—"piss over there, not here." Handwriting now gave me goosebumps. (My handwriting has stayed illegible to this day. In college, realizing my deficiency, I bought exercise books and practiced penmanship regularly for months, but to no effect.)

The thatch and bamboo school soon became uninhabitable. A village lunatic made the school his nightly home. He caught fish in the streams and brought them inside the school to roast and eat, soiling the place in the process. In the morning when we got there, the classrooms stank, his urine and feces and fishbones strewn everywhere. And then Hari's brother Radha died of rabies, barking like a dog. He had been bitten by a rabid dog on his way to school. The thatch-and-bamboo school was abandoned, and we moved for a few weeks to the barbers' huts in the bazaar.

This was when I had a brother born. Mai often looked up at the sky, and said, "God, you had fair clay only for me, not for my son." And now the same God had heard her prayer and sent a pale-skinned brother to me. In the second-grade textbook, I had read, "Binod is a good boy." Binod was both fair and good, like my brother. I named my brother Binod.

It doesn't matter if Pramod is "a restless monkey" or "a loser hare," the names boys called me from schoolbook stories. In the books, the monkey never got anything done and the hare always lost to the tortoise. My brother would be the winner tortoise and a normal boy when he grows up. Pramod–Binod. Bad–Good. Dark–Fair. Hare–Tortoise. But four months later, Binod caught a whizzing cough. Mai tried every remedy she could find in the village. The village shaman made a potion at the crossroads, mixing and heating on dry dung of a red cow, mustard oil, herbs, roots and witch-beating, and ghost-busting mantras. That, too, didn't work, and we took Binod to the nearest doctor in Rangeli, four hours south. The doctor gave an injection. When we returned home, Binod's cough worsened. Mai blamed a masseur woman who was charcoal black, possessed of big eyes and a flat nose. The woman swore she didn't do anything. She said she was no witch. Father said witchcraft is nothing but superstition. On the third day, Binod grew worse; his breathing slowed, then stopped altogether. Father wrapped Binod in a sheet and grabbed a hoe and headed for the marshes to bury him on its raised edge.

Around this time, Mai's bhaya (friend) in our adjacent courtyard died in childbirth. Bhaya Aai's husband's uncle, a renowned shaman, died when he couldn't urinate anymore. The villagers buried them on the side of the creek by the forest's edge and returned home. They blamed the evil spirits and ghosts that roamed the outskirts of the village and randomly picked anybody they liked or hated. Some of these spirits were called Gahili; others, Kali and Sansari. Frightened of ghosts and evil spirits in the village, and Mr. Sukna at school, dark clouds enveloped my soul.

> I realized that the black letters hid in them magic and wonders, the miraculous struggles between gods and demons—a world where I could be transported away from evil spirits, ghosts, and bullies, and my overall miserable past and present. The ultimate victory of gods over demons, of those who protect over those who harm, gave me hope.

The school had now moved back to the bazaar in a thatch and bamboo hut. The village elders collected the barks of Sal trees (shorea robusta) from the forest. And we again went around villages collecting thatch. Soon, the schoolhouse of bark wall and thatch roof stood a few yards west of our first one-room schoolhouse.

It turned out that the Headmaster, Sant Lal, was not "Matric Fail" as rumored but only "Eighth Fail." At a time when nobody in the villages had any completed formal educational degrees, we used "Matric Fail" and "B.A. Fail" as degree names for those who had spent the required time in school for the degree but failed. Since Sant Lal, Mr. Sukna, and Mr. Thtliwal had left by then, Mr. Dulal, who had come down from the hills, became our Headmaster. The rumor had it that he had completed "Normal Training," which sounded abnormal to us because he outlawed beating with a stick, and said, "Pulling the side hair is more than enough." We had heard "Matric Fail" and "IA Fail" (Intermediate in Arts) as degrees, but never Normal Training. This degree mightily impressed us all. My fear diminished a little.

One day, a young man appeared in the bazaar. He had well-combed, well-oiled hair, wore steel-framed glasses, clean and ironed, short-sleeve white shirt and pleated pants, and his teeth were brush-paste clean and white, unlike many of ours, as we either didn't brush our teeth at all, letting them turn yellow and gather green plaque in between the gums, or used only bamboo and twigs to fulfill the duty of our teeth-cleaning morning ritual. We were astonished when we heard him speak English. Until then, I thought English was something the spelling of whose words you memorized—"C-O-W, cow, cow means mooing gai;" "D-O-G, dog, dog means barking kukur"—while swinging your head and body back and forth, sitting on a mat at home or on the bench at school. This sharply dressed gentleman's name, we were told, was Prem Kumar. And he was said to be from Darjeeling. What is Darjeeling like, I wondered, where such well-dressed, well-fed men live? And his degree, too, was no less astonishing. He was I.A. Fail. Father heard about him and in no time sent Third-Grade-Fail me to him every morning for tutoring. Even this tutoring didn't do much good to me. My mind stayed distracted by fear of ghosts and bullies.

On another day, I came home early from my playing rounds in the village. I saw a brick-size book lying in a corner on Jahar Singh's verandah. (Jahar Singh, the Village Chief, lived in the same courtyard as we did and had by then become my social uncle; Mai called his wife, Bai—sister.) The book caught my eye, for I had never seen a book of that size. I approached it, furtively looking around lest anybody saw me, the failed boy, daring to get near the brick-size book. I looked at the cover. It had the picture of a thousand-headed snake and a flute-playing man riding its hood. I couldn't help turning the pages. Inserted in various places in the book were pictures of dreadlocked, bearded sages, bow-and-arrow, mace-wielding warriors, and fanged, horned demons, human bodies with heads of lions, eviscerating a demon and boar-man lifting the globe on its tusk. These pictures set my curiosity ablaze; I shivered with excitement to imagine what the black letters inside the book might hold. I worked hard to read the words and sentences, one word and sentence at a time. I don't know how or why Jahar Singh had bought the book, whose title said *Sukhsagar*.

By then I had already seen the epics—*Mahabharata* and *Ramayana*—performed by the Masunda dance troupes that came from across the borders from India on festivals. The characters spoke prose dialogue in Hindi but sang the verses in Bengali. The distant familiarity with Hindi also helped me comprehend the book's sentences. The book had the story of King Parikshit who was under a curse to die by snake bite within seven days. Frightened, the king assembled the wisest of the sages and asked them to show him a way to escape the curse. Only Sukdev Muni, they said, could show him the way. I was astonished to see a picture of Sukdev Muni when he appeared in the palace. He was a boy of seven, my age, and blessed to remain seven forever, but the seven-year-old knew all about the universe, its beginnings and endings.

While I was tickled to know the sage to be my age and all-knowing, I felt shame to find myself a know-nothing who couldn't pass even third grade. To top it all, the sage knew the way out of death, but here I was frightened by death's claws picking out one person after another around me. The book took hold of me as nothing before. I forgot to eat. Waking, sleeping, cow herding, I carried the book and read wherever and whenever I could. Mai saw me lost in the book, and said, "I don't see you reading your schoolbook anymore. If you don't watch out, boy, you will fail again. 'Mother's a maid; the son's name is Durga Dutt.'" The proverb about the mother and her pretentious, profligate son remained her favorite recital all through my childhood.

Husking rice, stirring the sand and rice puffs in the clay pot on the mud stove, boiling milk, and doing her chores, Mai's warning never ceased. To escape her sharp tongue and watchful eyes, I read the book secretly, in the cow shed loft, and carried the book in a sack in the harvested fields and the forest where I let the herd loose. I realized that the black letters hid in them magic and wonders, the miraculous struggles between gods and demons—a world where I could be transported away from evil spirits, ghosts, and bullies, and my overall miserable past and present. The ultimate victory of gods over demons, of those who protect over those who harm, gave me hope. To be like Sukdev meant I could escape even death. If Sukdev could be everyone's revered figure, why could I remain everybody's butt of insult and denigration? The cells of my mind awakened. Prem Kumar's English lessons took on life and light. Even though my handwriting still looked like crow legs, the speed of my writing quickened. Culturally sanctioned early morning lessons hardly registered in my mind, but the day learning from reading the book sank into my soul.

In the Half-Yearly exam, Mr. Dulal, the Headmaster, promoted me to the fourth grade. I caught up with my classmates. The bullies no longer pestered me with "Naughty Monkey" or "Loser Hare" or "Pot Breaker." Instead, they gave me a new sobriquet—"Promoted"—which jibed with my name. But I could care less now what the bullies or the world called me. My goal now was the story's sage, Sukdev Muni. To be like him. I was beginning to feel what it meant to be human. In six months, the final exams came with the yellowing of the rice paddies. When I wrote my fourth-grade exams, the ink smeared all over my fingers. When the results were announced, I stood first in the entire school. Father was once again on his travels in India. When I returned home with a bucket full of prizes of notebooks and pens, and my neck and shoulders loaded with flowers, Mai couldn't help her tears of joy.

This crucial awakening opened a world for me that inspired me to read and write. In the absence of adequate means to travel distances, books helped me expand my imagination. When challenges confronted me in later years, the inspiration and motivation that I continued to derive from reading helped sustain my faith in life and life's endless possibilities. And books, reading, and writing still give me meaning and sustenance. Those earlier years when I was going through school, college, and universities in India and Nepal were challenging years, but that early spark of childhood kept the flame alive and helped me overcome challenges that awaited me later in life.

Many challenges—personal, financial, and social—have come my way since that early encounter with the inspiring narrator in the book called *Sukhsagar*. But the inspiration to learn and spread learning remained a constant goal in my life. And that inspiration paved the way for my vocation. I believe that each one of us has our own way of coming upon our vocation. Mine came after considerable hardship. But ultimately, I can say that I feel blessed that I found mine.

The United States Flag and Me

by Roman Ortega, Jr., M.B.A.

Class of '13
Associate Vice President for Strategy (Formerly Employed)
Lieutenant Colonel, United States Army

The Flag and Patriotism

The hours I spent wearing the vest, always knowing that the flag contained within it, by my heart, would be draped at my funeral. The constant reminder of mortality, and how in war you have to embrace it in order to lead, or the sheer violence will paralyze you. You must get a hold of the fear and convert it into a power source that will energize success on the battlefield.

In many ways, I felt destined to be a Soldier. Heck, it is right in my name: I was named after Romulus, the founder and King of Rome, the creator of one of the greatest armies that the world has ever known. I felt drawn to the military because it offered structure, order, discipline, and people working towards a common goal. I enjoyed the physical nature of the Army: You must be fit if you want to be part of the organization. But to be as stellar a Soldier as you could be meant being physically, emotionally, mentally, and spiritually balanced. The Army also allows you to release your primal nature by fighting and training as a warrior. Some of the most challenging training I experienced, in Ranger School—the Army's elite military leadership course, one of the toughest around the world—feeds into the nature of being a Soldier that fights and wins the nation's wars. As they say in the Ranger Creed: "I shall defeat them on the field of battle for I am better trained and will fight with all my might. Surrender is not a Ranger word."

Growing Up: Unprotected

As a young child, I felt loved by my family, but I also understood that our family was different compared to those families who were not immigrants, did not lack resources, who spoke the language—that is, families that had a social safety net. Many families living in Cicero, Illinois, came from humble beginnings and were immigrants like my parents. They worked multiple jobs to make ends meet. Their drive to provide a stable home kept them out of the house, working long shifts, which often left me leaving the house alone and coming home alone. I understood that this was necessary, but it also made me sad. I was bullied and physically assaulted many times as a child, and more often than not from many kids at one time. I recall many times walking home alone, bloodied and bruised, to come home to an empty house. Because my parents were not home, I was not protected, but even as a child I understood why. My family needed to work in order to thrive. They also lacked the understanding of what life was like in America, and it was foreign to them that people would be so cruel. For many years as a young child, I was also subject to abuse from extended family and the community. I was abused and harmed without fully understanding why that was my situation. I saw that my cousins and friends were not being treated poorly, and I didn't know why or how I was different.

It was not until adulthood that I realized my mannerisms and demeanor were the reasons I was perceived as different. My demeanor is formal, exact, organized, and fast-paced. Even as a child I tended to be constantly thinking and lost in thought. As an adult, I have found a way to successfully hone those skills and be self-aware enough to understand that I lean towards formality versus an easy-going nature. The nature of how I operate, sometimes thought of as methodical, stems from a need to be in control to avoid my environment controlling me. I lacked control as a child,

and I was determined to gain control of my life and not be embarrassed of my humble beginnings, different mannerisms, and weaker physical attributes. That violence and trauma shaped me to want to no longer be seen as weak and to be able to protect others from harm. So, naturally, I joined the world's most advanced military into a branch and job that is one of the most challenging in the world. I was determined to prove my toughness and resilience, that I could persevere even when others counted me out. As an adult, I have used my mental wiring to my advantage—to constantly learn, understand how to lead others, and ensure never to fail my teammates.

My Path to Service

Many experiences informed the type of person I wanted to be, and ultimately it was someone that was of service to others—in particular, a service in the armed forces that supported and defended the U.S. Constitution and freedoms of those who could not. My path to service is similar to many other service members from immigrant families. I was raised with this idea that the United States provided a framework to allow people to flourish if they worked hard and did the right thing. Considering the humble beginnings that my parents came from in Mexico to what they've been able to achieve financially, professionally, and overall regarding their own freedom, they have accomplished more than they would have in any other country. My father was the first of ten brothers and sisters in a remote part of Mexico. At that time, the pueblo contained two-hundred inhabitants, with no running water, electricity, or heat. He was born in a shelter made out of rocks, and it was not until he became older that he had a traditional shelter that he helped build. He didn't have many opportunities to thrive in Mexico, and at the young age of seventeen, he decided to come to the United States illegally. His first day at the border attempt to cross was fraught with an inability to cross because of border security. He found himself sleeping on the streets and not eating from a lack of money. By the grace of God, a taco vendor gave my father food until he was able to cross the border. A few years later, my father was able to repay the taco vendor the amount owed and then some.

My mother also grew up with a large family of ten brothers and sisters and was primarily raised by her mother because she lost her father at a young age. She also came to the United States illegally, crossing the Rio Grande on a play-inflatable tube. On the first attempt, they were caught by the border patrol and taken into custody. I have been told that if the border patrol did not capture them, the smuggler getting them over the river would have robbed and left them in desolate conditions. After that initial capture, they decided, out of desperation, to attempt the crossing again, and this time they were successful. While both my parents lacked a traditional education, resources, or a network, they managed a way to thrive and preserve themselves in life. This narrative

and their experience compelled me to give back to a country that enabled my family to succeed, be educated, and have a sustainable quality of life.

I also recognize that the U.S. military offered many benefits for service—not only civil service but also the ability to afford college. I knew I wanted to attend college, but it was not clear how I would afford it. To have the freedom to make a decision to go to college without feeling financially burdened, I discerned that the military was a good way to achieve this goal. The G.I. Bill wasn't the only reason I joined the military, but it *was* a reason. The physical and "manly" aspects of the combat arms also resonated with me. I wanted to show that I was physically tough and could be an elite soldier that should not be messed with.

Finally, I was raised by a common philosophy of resilience to persevere under the most challenging situations and achieve success. Both the Mexican spirit and American spirit embody this ideology of resilience. And I believed serving in the military was a grand equalizer to achieving the American dream. Military service offered job experience, access to the G.I. Bill to support attaining a college degree, and a common pride that Americans have for the military. Ultimately, a sense of service to the country—defense of our country and others—became my calling.

Now, looking back on it, my original time for entrance into the military is quite laughable. I innocently walked into the recruiter's office and said I wanted to sign

> **"**
> I was determined to prove my toughness and resilience—
> that I could persevere even when others counted me
> out. As an adult, I have used my mental wiring to my
> advantage—to constantly learn, understand how to lead
> others, and ensure never to fail my teammates.
> **"**

up, with no idea what my job would be, when I would leave, or what my service would really entail. Well, they needed an infantryman, and they signed me right up. I didn't question it and soon found myself serving as a mortarman in the infantry. A mortarman is an infantryman who carries small bombs on their back and launches them when fighting the enemy; it lacks glamour and is physically punishing, carrying 100-plus pounds on your back for days on end. The infantry and other combat-related jobs are where wars are won and ultimately ended; it is the most challenging job in the military and, by nature, the most impactful. It requires a certain level of discipline, physical resolve, emotional toughness, and a sense of duty to serve on the front lines. It was not that I was not intelligent enough to serve in other military specialties, but more so that I wanted to be where war was waged and won. Looking back on it, I absolutely loved the infantry, and once I became an army officer, I felt compelled to join the infantry again.

After my time in the service, I attended Northern Illinois University (NIU) using my G.I. Bill. During my time at NIU, while in the reserves at the same time, I decided that I wanted to go back to active duty, but this time as an army officer. I had been inspired by infantry officers in the military, and I wanted to become one. I also recognized that while the military was a diverse and inclusive organization, there weren't many people in leadership roles within the officer ranks that looked, spoke, and had the same cultural background that I did. I saw many soldiers in the enlisted ranks that looked like me and came from the same background. I saw many people of color in the enlisted ranks but not many as military officers. I didn't necessarily want to be a role model, but I did want people like me to be represented in the leadership ranks. I felt that I could be a leader who represented my ethnicity as a Mexican American. The culture of the military empowered me to become a military officer. And my values as a Mexican American would serve as an example to the soldiers in the enlisted ranks. I now have more than twenty-six years of military service, with the current rank of Lieutenant Colonel, and I still feel the same pull of wanting to proudly represent my ethnicity as a Mexican American.

The Iraq War

Before I deployed to Iraq, I decided to bring my American flag with me, to place it into my vest, to serve as a constant reminder of what it meant to me. I wore this flag at all times—while on patrol, while in combat, while I slept, while I mourned. It is the flag that my children will bury me in, and the flag that I would be injured in during the war. It is the flag that reminds me of the freedom that I have earned for my family, the flag that would remind me of the better life that my parents were able to attain because of it. It is the flag that reminds me that we are a young nation that has made mistakes, and that I, too, would make some mistakes while being a leader. It is the flag that reminds me of the sorrow I felt while wearing it, like when we would lose a Soldier, and when my father was diagnosed with cancer while I was away at war. The flag now sits in my home as an omnipresent object that reminds me of a long time ago when life was, at times, bleak but also simple. It also reminds me of the behavioral health sacrifice I made while wearing it.

The time in the war was a difficult and life-changing experience for me. It was tough to see the good in life; I lost many friends in extremely violent ways. War makes people question their humanity and what their role is in the world, to build a more just and verdant world. I understood war to be many shades of gray, and not black and white, around what is wrong and what is right. At first glance, you might say that the enemy is the terrorist putting in a roadside bomb, but as you dig deeper, you realize that that person who put it in was merely being paid by a large organization to emplace a bomb because they were compelled to provide for their families. Some subscribe to the rhetoric of a radical religious ideology that is not in keeping with the normative understanding of the religion and thus feel justified in the violent actions they take. On the other hand, an altruistic soldier might go overseas to fight thinking there is going to be a clear delineation of who the enemy is and assume what he, the soldier, is doing will build stability in the area. But at times, all those efforts can be lost due to political instability and the lack of intentionality and motivation by the leaders or the population of a certain country. In fact, the soldier's actions can be at times looked at as if the actions had no purpose and perhaps created even more instability due to violence. For me, I like to think that I made a difference, and if nothing else, that I tried my best to lead my soldiers to the best of my capabilities, and that I showed humanity at the most challenging times and conditions.

My time in Iraq was fraught with much internal struggle. I saw many people in dire circumstances because of a failed political regime in Saddam Hussain. As American soldiers, our time would bring stability to a war-torn country by rebuilding the infrastructure needed to be a flourishing country again. At the same time, I wondered if the actions, violence, and developments by the United States were only hindering progress—the infrastructure being built that a war-torn country would not sustain after the Americans left, the long-term trauma caused by war being waged around Iraqi society. How much of what we did was a hero complex that we could go in and save the day? Was all the death and trauma worth it?

I remember smells and feelings more than memories of images. The scents of streets riddled with garbage, feces, and burning rubber. The scents sear your nostrils as if going so deep into your body that they become part of your DNA. The smell of carbon dissipating in the air after a violent explosion or a fired rifle that awakens the senses. The polyurethane that coats the top of my bulletproof plates placed within my vest that seemingly emits a smell in the 120-plus degree heat. The trauma of the war blocked many of my memories, but the smell and emotions are as vibrant as the day they happened. And in a way, just as I struggled as a child, feeling like I didn't belong in the United States, I was feeling like an American who didn't belong in Iraq. The irony was not lost on me—feeling like a foreigner growing up as an outsider within the United States, and then, voluntarily, as a foreigner in a war-torn country. In both instances, I did belong. I was born in the United States as a citizen, and I was serving in Iraq, part of a campaign to free oppressed Iraqi people.

Struggle with the War

Anyone who tells you that the war left them without scars is lying. Sometimes people in extreme conditions like the front line of war are required to do things that should not be done. War brings out the most extreme conditions and the most extreme of decisions. Even if you do not serve on the front lines, you are left with the scars of being away from family for such an extended period, the isolation, the constant high-pressure environment, the threat of rockets, mortars, or other projectiles constantly threatening you on a base that you think is secured. Sometimes the most damaging scars are the ones unseen, the ones that leave an undeniable mark in the recesses of your mind. For me, it was the conduct of death all around, whether that was insurgents killing innocent people in a marketplace, the killing of an insurgent emplacing a roadside bomb, or finding mass graves of innocent people killed in sectarian violence. The images, smells, and thoughts cause scars on the mind from an extreme of humanity, which is devoid of humanity in how we treat each other.

Suppose the unseen scars go untreated. They fester like a wound that becomes infected. Eventually, the infection grows and envelopes your life in such a way that you lose your behavioral health. A remedy to help treat the wounds is through mental health support by professionals and families. It has been my experience that those who have support systems can deal with the chaos and ultimately flourish after the war. Those who go untreated end up having unhealthy lives and, at times, end their lives. I have lost more soldiers after the war due to suicide than I lost during the war to combat injuries. And then there's the ripple effects that suicide or death have on families and loved ones. I found myself in the mental health department of Walter Reed hospital, contemplating ending my life because I was struggling to adapt to my new, non-war environment. It wasn't only the war that I was working with, but also a poor marriage and a newborn child that I didn't know. I felt like they wanted nothing to do with me and the stress of serving in an army still at war. I was fortunate enough to get help at the right time and receive the resources to heal and eventually flourish. It is now part of my vocation to support others in need and advocate for mental health support.

Time with Lewis

Lewis offered me an opportunity to continue to serve, grow professionally, and positively impact the lives of others—a continuation of service and fulfillment of my vocation. My role as the Director of Veterans Affairs began with supporting Veterans in the greater military community, helping Veterans of all genders, races, ethnicities, and backgrounds to be re-engaged, accepted, supported, and empowered to grow and succeed. As the Executive Director of International and Military Affairs (and later as Executive Director of University Advancement and Government Relations and Associate Vice President for Strategy), the work expanded to other areas that are of great importance to me, those being diversity, equity, and inclusion of other underserved and marginalized populations. We now have over one-thousand international students attending the University, which was part of a shared vision to help expand the horizons of all our students and understand the interconnectedness of all humans around the globe.

The "High" of Commitment

by Michael L. Parker. B.A.

Class of '77
Board Chair of the Lewis University Board of Trustees

A crowded gathering place and the familiar din of a huge crowd, stoked in the anticipation of what is to come next. For many of us in the procession, this is a bi-annual event, but for many of those traversing the platform, this is a once-in-a-lifetime moment. I can hear the robust tones of "Pomp and Circumstance." The richness of the horns and the staccato roll of the drums resonate throughout the cavernous space, chock full of proud people. The black caps and gowns of the graduates contrast with the brightly colored gowns adorning many of those who have helped make this fine moment possible—faculty, staff, and trustees. The creative decorations and declarations on the otherwise plain mortarboards draw my attention, but nothing is more pronounced and radiant than the smiles of anticipation on the faces of parents and loved ones who grace the assembly. Yes, let there be no doubt, I am speaking of the ritual of college graduation. No matter how many times I attend, this is never perfunctory. This never gets old.

As a University trustee, I am in the processional group that enters the assembly last. After we slowly walk down the aisle, we ascend the five steps to the platform, locate our seats, and directly face both the bright lights as well as those who are in such wonderful anticipation. That is when I am drawn to ask myself, "Did I do everything I could do to help them?" This question comes not from a feeling of guilt. I believe it is the underpinnings of real commitment.

Though my childhood was not exemplary, all the same I had some wonderful moments. Some of my most amazing and memorable moments include traveling on vacation with my grandparents nearly every summer, always in a Ford Country Squire station wagon, city to city, state to state, with a full complement of geographical trivia to and from our destination to stave off any possibility of boredom. We visited relatives and friends like us, from limited means, with a zest for life and family closeness that was unparalleled. This is where I would learn lessons about social justice, race relations, discrimination, and social acceptance. I would also learn about the artistry and value of the personal relationship and how the personal relationship is the equalizer in social and even business settings. These important lessons became one of the building blocks of my persona. They heightened my ability to be motivated in the light of the difficult social pressures in my school environment and my neighborhood.

My relationship with my mother and my maternal grandparents helped to mold me into the resilient person I am today. Growing up the product of a broken home presented challenges. The truth of the matter is that even before our home was broken, there were gaping tears in the fabric of our family because of the absence of our father. These were both financial and emotional. Mom and dad separated and reunited, then separated and reunited. Each time, she separated because of the toll on her, then reunited because of the toll on us children. After a strained year of residence in Colorado, we moved in with our grandparents so that mom could reestablish employment. We had changed our state of residence during one of the reunions, but nothing had changed regarding the dynamics of the union. Because of the amount of financial pressure my mother experienced raising three boys, I learned to contribute to the family as much as I could. I turned into the "man" of the house. I tried to fix everything mechanical, do the landscaping, and from seventh grade on, do my part to protect my mother and

my younger brother from the extremes of our south-end-of-Joliet neighborhood. At the same time, I learned to be nearly stoical about the things that were missing; because my mother worked so hard to give us what she could, it would be grossly unfair to ever complain.

There is an art to raising children so filled with love and curiosity that they don't know that the available resources that underpin them are quite limited. Those three—my mother, grandfather, and grandmother—figured out how to do it. My mother was a hard-working civil service employee at the Joliet Arsenal. My grandfather was an amazing teacher at a reform school. And my grandmother was the ultimate household "engineer." We were taught to be socially conscious, fair, resilient, hardworking, and loving. For example, all three focused on our being good citizens. In grade school, we labored in a bountiful garden and shared fresh produce with our neighbors. It was hard to think about what we lacked when we were enjoying helping others. We developed a sense of empathy as we were overcome with how much it was appreciated, and it brought us closer to others. We were also the beneficiaries of having a master teacher as a grandfather, whose boundless energy was directed at our enlightenment. My mother and grandparents also provided for us an assembly of books that would make a library jealous. We read incessantly, from comic books to classics. This reading stimulated my older brother and me to a degree that movies at the theater could be a letdown. Also, their insistence and support of our involvement with youth sports gave us grade school years that were so memorable. And they played board games with us weekly, which generated a closeness that I tried to duplicate with my children and grandchildren.

From the time when we were quite young, the question was not *whether* we would go to college, but *where* we would go. After a few years of living with my wonderful grandparents, we moved in with our mother in Joliet. During these high school years, my older brother (one year older) and I were faced with the task of figuring out how we might pay for college. Both of us had some athletic ability, and with hard work and with the grace of God, we were able to pay for college by means of basketball scholarships.

My brother went to the University of Iowa on a basketball scholarship. A year later, Lewis University recruited me to play basketball, and my choice of Lewis gave me the ability to live close to my grandparents, who lived about twenty-five miles from campus, and not too far from my mother, who had relocated to work at the Rock Island Arsenal. What I did not know was that the molding process was still taking shape. I knew nothing of the tenets of a Lasallian education. I was not aware of the mission of the University. As a matter of fact, I don't believe anyone even tried to relate it to me. What I knew was that the dream, and in my case, the obligation, of getting an education was now going to be financed.

I showed up on the Lewis University campus in August of 1973. It took me just a few weeks to recognize that I had made a good choice. If I recall correctly, Lewis had about 2,200 students, and that was a fine size. What was more important and meaningful to me was that the staff and faculty began to nurture me. I took this opportunity and their nurturing seriously, and I began to work as hard as possible. At the same time, I began to realize my true potential away from the basketball court.

At Lewis, I had solid mentors and informal "advisors"—caring individuals who helped to shape my college experience from the very beginning. The Dean of Students, Tom Kennedy, was especially helpful, as was the Director of Minority Affairs, Dr. Charles Kennedy. They both gave me valuable guidance all the way through my education. The Director of the College Success program, Kathleen Bolden, was a constant contributor to my university and life experiences, even though I was not in her program. When I struggled financially, Ms. Bolden gave me my first work-study employment as a Peer Group Counselor, helping other students navigate the university's maze of resources. The income was helpful in my quests to remain independent and not be a burden on my mother. I can visualize some of our conversations right now. Her insights were invaluable as she consistently helped me to steer around obstacles educationally and in life. And my favorite English professor, Brother Urban Lucken, took critical interest in my writings. I can hear his voice right now in his special way of complimenting me without letting me get ahead of myself. I still have some of the papers he critiqued for me. Each of these individuals took time to understand my situation and to offer guidance, not just to me, but also to other students who needed help.

When I made the difficult decision to get married at the young age of twenty, and needed to accelerate my studies, the Department Chair of Political Science, Dr. Joseph Gaziano, and my Economics Professor, Dr. Larry Hill, each allowed me to take a class as independent study, which allowed me to graduate early and begin the job of supporting my small family. Couple this with the sincere backing of my basketball coach, Tony Delgado, and Athletic Director, Gordie Gillespie, as they both supported me without question. With the help of all these fine individuals, I knew I would succeed. All of this was possible because professors, administrators, and staff took time to know me. They obviously cared, and I was so fortunate to be the beneficiary.

I graduated in December of 1976 with a degree in Public Administration, the very first Public Administration major to graduate from Lewis University. And then, five months later, in May of 1977, I had the good fortune to begin working for the company I eventually retired from. In 2009, I was named General Manager, Executive Vice President for Field Operations for this $1.6 billion dollar company—the pinnacle of my wonderful career. I retired in 2010.

In 2004, I joined the Lewis University Board of Trustees. I could not have been more proud. Lewis had been good to me, and good *for* me. Now, I was going to be able to give something back! In the most heartfelt and genuine way, I have empathy for young people who are struggling. So many come from single-parent, female-led families, just like I did. So many are of limited means but are buoyed by the hopes of a family that loves them, just like me. So many are going to be the examples for their younger siblings as they attempt to find success in college and employment. These accomplishments will set the bar for the family and for the future. They are just like me, and I was just like them! My sensitivity to their journey to get to college, their struggles while at the University, as well as their plight once they graduate, is so much like what I remember from my journey. I sense their burdens. The struggle is real, and they deserve help. Quietly, I want to do just that.

There's something of a catharsis when you do even small things that help to change someone's life. These acts might not seem significant until later in their lives. You have to have faith.

In 2008, my wife, Angelique, and I gave a lump sum of money to the University to start an endowed scholarship in our name to support a scholarship every year for Black or Latino students. Creating this scholarship is something that I will never regret. A year later, in 2009, I knew that I could do more. I was able to augment the original offering to ease the financial burdens of some great students by inviting students to submit essay applications for four scholarships. Two of the students per year are provided scholarships from the Michael L. Parker and Angelique M. Parker Black Student Union (BSU) Scholarship. Two more fine students are annually awarded scholarships from the Michael L. Parker and Angelique M. Parker Gospel Choir Scholarship. Financially assisting a total of five deserving students annually in covering the costs of their education felt fulfilling.

An important part of the process, we agreed that I would personally present four of the scholarships. I would get to see the faces of the students as they receive their scholarships. The BSU Scholarship would be given first, at the Black Heritage Ball, normally held during Black History Month (February). The scholarships that would go to the Gospel Choir members would be given later at Gospel Fest, a gathering of the Lewis Gospel Choir and several other gospel groups from around the Chicago area.

I brimmed with anticipation as we came upon the date of the Black Heritage Ball. I was to present my first two scholarships to two deserving students. You could hear a pin drop in the room. I could tell that this really meant something to these deserving students. There were students, a few parents, and some guests present. When I read the name of the first recipient, there was a shriek! It was the scholarship recipient reacting with joy and disbelief to being chosen. The crowd reacted with applause as she came to the front and gave me nothing less than a bear hug. When I read the next name, the student was not present; she was representing the University at an athletic event. The crowd was pleased for her and applauded energetically. During the program, someone called the young woman about the scholarship. She asked to speak to me by mobile phone at the end of the program. It was obvious that being chosen excited her. She said: "Mr. Parker, you don't know how much I needed this! Thank you for selecting me!" I was overcome. I neglected to tell her that I don't have any role in selecting the recipients. Frankly, she could not have been happier about it than I was!

One of the fine students that received a Black Student Union Scholarship graduated from the University in 2015. She was a wonderful student who so appreciated getting the scholarship in her all-important senior year. As we neared graduation time, she sent me an email and asked if I would attend her pinning ceremony for graduating nursing students. She indicated that she really wanted me to be there and that I would be able to meet her mother. I was flattered, and I certainly agreed. As luck would have it, the week prior to the pinning, I underwent major surgery. My recovery was going well, and I decided that I needed to honor my commitment, much to the admonitions of my wife. When I arrived at the pinning, one of the University Advancement staff kindly assisted me because of my condition and seated me in the front row. I witnessed the pinning and was nearly as proud as the student's mother, who coincidentally sat right behind me. She let her tears flow, and I did all that I could do to hold mine back. That wonderful student is now an operating room nurse at Rush-Presbyterian St. Luke's Hospital.

Helping these fine students is a dream. By my cursory estimation, since starting this in 2008, I have had the pleasure of funding more than sixty-four scholarships for the Parker Endowed Scholarship, the Black Student Union, and the Gospel Choir. More importantly, some of the students were multiple-year recipients. Some students have accepted the presentation of their scholarship award in tears, but most accept with broad smiles across their faces. The feelings of appreciation are palpable.

Real, everyday students are the objective. I did not want the construction of my scholarship program to require an inordinately high GPA or some difficult-to-sustain standards. Many of these students have seen enough barriers to educational success all their educational lives. Years later, the successes are evident. Many early recipients are now in solid positions: associate vice presidents, clinical nurses, social workers, directors, higher education professionals, aviation managers, air traffic controllers, and so many more. Many have gone on to get graduate degrees as well. Numerous recent grads are learning their trade in their entry-level positions. Whatever yardstick you use to measure, these students are finding success. Helping these amazing students and seeing them face-to-face creates a "high," a high that is infectious and self-sustaining. As they experience success, I experience success.

With the graduation remarks concluding, I quickly look to the program for the two "Parker" scholarship recipients on the graduation program. I'm excited to be present for their walk across the platform. I told them that, if possible, I would recognize them on their big day!

After seeing a myriad of students traverse the platform, my anticipation is building. As each of them come across, receive their diploma, and shake hands with the Dean, Board Chair, and University President, I move from my seat on the platform and walk toward them and harvest a huge hug—the kind of hug that assures you that you not only did the right thing, but that "thing" you did was really appreciated. Both say, "Thank you so much, Mr. Parker!" That dividend is so reinforcing, so energizing. As we exit the field house, I feel, well, like I have made a difference. That is an overwhelmingly good feeling.

I know I am following my internal compass if I continue to ask myself the most salient question: *"Did I do everything I could do?"*

The Unexpected Journey

by Michael Progress, M.B.A., M.A.

Class of '92, '96, '01, '13, '16, and '22
Assistant Dean, College of Business

If you would have asked me as a child what I wanted to be when I grew up, working in a college setting would never have crossed my mind. During my early school years, I dreaded school, especially when I was in kindergarten. I lived only three houses down from my grade school, but when I was there, I felt like I was so far away from home. Each academic year seemed to get a little better. It was only when I got into high school that I truly started to enjoy school. It is strange how life's twists and turns can lead and call us to unexpected places and vocations.

I was raised in the small, rural town of Seneca, Illinois, with a population of just over 2,000 people. There were fifty-nine students in my graduating high school class. Prior to starting high school, the high school principal visited each of our homes. The main street had no traffic lights, just one stop sign at the north end. It was thirteen miles to the nearest major retailer. I believe growing up in such a small town had a huge impact on my life decisions, especially the ones I had to make in my late teenage years and early twenties. Decisions of where to attend college, what size college, what career to prepare for during college, where I envisioned living after college, were all based on the impressions and information I had at that time and my experiences of growing up in a small town.

I would definitely say my early life experiences of growing up in a small town are the main reason I decided to attend Lewis University. Lewis met all my needs, was just far enough away from my home, and small enough that I felt that I would not get lost in the crowd. To be perfectly honest, being non-Catholic was one of my only real concerns. Would I fit in at Lewis, being non-Catholic? Before my freshman year ended, in the spring of 1988, that concern had long disappeared. In fact, in an ironic twist, I ended up being a student worker for University Ministry. Additionally, I was a member of Lewis University's very first *Koinonia,* a weekend retreat open to all students designed to help students discover themselves and God.

As an undergraduate, I first majored in accounting. I selected this major strictly on career outlook, anticipated compensation, and the fact that I enjoyed the accounting-related courses that I took in high school. All started off well, but by the end of my first semester, I realized accounting was not the major for me. For me, the prospects of being able to secure a great paying job in the accounting field did not outweigh the thought of sitting at a desk for the vast majority of the day. Not that there is anything wrong with that—I just could not imagine being in that type of work environment for the next thirty or forty years.

In the second semester of my first year in college, I ended up taking a basic marketing course. During this time, I quickly developed an interest in marketing. Being an introvert, and always associating marketing strictly with sales, I had never considered or explored any careers related to marketing. It was not until I learned that there were so many other areas of marketing besides sales that I considered it—advertising, marketing research, public relations, branding, and international marketing, to name just a few. Even before I finished the basic marketing course, I realized marketing was the major for me. I believe the main factor in my confidence of having selected the "right" major was that I had added my long-term happiness, strengths, and skills into the decision-making process for selecting a major. Marketing allowed me to use the creative side of my brain, giving me the opportunity to take a vision and make it into a tangible promotional piece. I truly enjoyed being a marketing major. If I had to do it all over again, I would still select marketing or digital marketing as my major.

I had the unfortunate luck of graduating from college during an economic recession—not a good experience. Looking for a position, for months, did nothing for my self-confidence. In hindsight, although an unpleasant experience, I used the time to reflect and reassess what I really wanted in life. During this time, I realized my desire to be geographically close to my family. I also realized living in a small town had its advantages and that I would actually prefer living in a smaller town.

Returning home after an interview—which I knew did not go well—I stopped by Lewis. One of my friends was working in the admissions office at the time. After I got done telling her about my latest interview experience, she mentioned Lewis had an opening in their business office. Being somewhat of a distance from my home, I had never even thought about exploring career opportunities at Lewis. Learning more about the position and benefits, I decided to apply.

At the time, I had been thinking about pursuing my master's in business administration degree. I thought taking evening courses while already being on campus during the day for work would be very convenient. Luckily, I was offered the position. I began working half-way during a fall semester, and I started my MBA the following spring. To be honest, my plan at the time was to gain a couple years of work experience, complete my MBA, and start searching for a career in the corporate world.

This first position at Lewis was in the accounts payable/receivable areas, which entailed processing incoming payments along with making sure all the financial obligations got paid. Luckily, I was not tied to a desk for the entire day. Sixty percent of my workweek involved working at the business office front service windows, working directly with students and other departments on campus. Through this work, I learned that I truly enjoyed working with students and being in a university setting. Also, looking back, I was fortunate to have a supervisor who was very student/customer-service focused.

After being in that position for eighteen months, I was contacted about a very good internal position, to serve as an Assistant Director of the Graduate School of Management. The only downside was that the position was on the Lewis University Schaumburg campus. If I were to apply and get the position, it would involve a 150-mile round-trip commute. After much reflection, I decided to apply for the position. I figured the opportunity to gain more higher education work experience far outweighed the negative of the long commute from Seneca to Schaumburg. Shortly after applying, I was offered, and I accepted, the Assistant Director position. It was a wonderful personal and career experience. The position gave me an opportunity to sharpen my professional skills. Like with my business office position, I was fortunate to have a supervisor who was an awesome mentor. The position also provided me with the opportunity to work more closely with faculty on things like course scheduling, prospective student recruitment initiatives, and student concerns. I realized that one of my favorite duties was acting as a liaison between students and faculty. I felt great satisfaction in helping students who were having some type of difficulty resolve their situation and continue their education. I received the same satisfaction helping faculty.

About six months after starting this position, I was diagnosed with cancer. At the beginning of my cancer experience, I did not know the extent of the cancer. Was it contained, or would the doctors find that it had spread to other areas? Luckily, after surgery and six weeks of radiation therapy, I was cancer-free and back to work. My experience with cancer was an opportunity for self-reflection, to stop and think about my mortality. Being only in my twenties, I am not sure if I would have done this reflecting—reflecting on what I held important and what I wanted to do with my life—if it had not been for my cancer diagnosis. For me, it drove home the importance of not taking life for granted. When making decisions, both small and large, I had a totally different perspective. Knowing there is no promise for tomorrow, even with being in my twenties, somehow

> For me, it drove home the importance of not taking life for granted.... Knowing there is no promise for tomorrow, even with being in my twenties, somehow provided clarity on the importance of the things and people around me.

provided clarity on the importance of the things and people around me.

During this time, I realized that I no longer had any desire to pursue corporate-related positions. I knew that I would be happier working within higher education. Looking back, I believe this is when I clearly realized my calling: helping students with their academic journeys. Along with this calling was also a desire to be a life-long learner. At this point, knowing I was going to remain in higher education, I started a graduate counseling psychology degree. I figured it would be a good degree should I ever want to move into some type of academic or career service-related position. I stayed in the Assistant Director position for a total of three years, when another internal position presented itself.

This next position would involve working in the registrar's office, serving as the Assistant Registrar. If I were hired for this position, I would still be working with students and faculty, but it would eliminate the longer commute since it was located on Lewis' Romeoville campus. Long story short, I applied and was offered the position. Again, as with my other two positions, I had a wonderful supervisor, an alumnus of Lewis who had been working for the University for many years. Working with him was a unique opportunity to gain knowledge of the University's history.

My primary role in this position was conducting final evaluations on graduating students' records, which provided an opportunity both to learn the various curricula across the University and to work with and get to know faculty throughout Lewis. Additionally, I often worked with several other administrative departments on campus. During my time in the registrar's office, I also finished my graduate counseling psychology degree.

Just when I was starting to think about something more challenging, the College of Business Assistant Dean position became available. From seeing the position through my eyes both as a student and as a former Graduate School of Management staff member, I thought it would be an interesting position—a nice mix of all the things I enjoyed. I would be able to continue to interact daily with students, and the other responsibilities like course scheduling and contracts would appeal to my love of organization and detail. Not knowing when I would ever have a chance to apply again, I decided to apply. As with my previous positions, my supervisor was supportive of this growth opportunity and encouraged me. (Looking back, hopefully they were not just wanting to get rid of me.)

As faith would have it, I was offered the Assistant Dean position, the position that I still hold today. Being an alumnus of the College of Business and having already worked in their graduate area was like coming full circle—or home. Over the last seventeen years, my current position has allowed me to work with so many wonderful individuals. I have learned so much, from both faculty and students. And my time at Lewis continues to fuel my love for life-long learning, having earned two additional bachelor's degrees, one in General Studio Art and the other in Social Media Marketing, along with starting a third graduate degree in Business Analytics. As challenging as balancing work, school, and personal responsibilities can be, I find them all rewarding.

One of things I love most about this position is that no two days are ever really the same. When I walk through the front door, I never know what new challenge is going to present itself. Through my journey, I feel that I am truly in a place to practice my vocation—helping others, enjoying life-long learning, being able to be ethically grounded, and feeling that I am making a difference in the world.

Finding Passion and Exploring True Self

by Iyad Rock, M.B.A.

Class of '15
Instructor, Department of Accounting

Guidance, reflection, intervention, and direction. These words describe my journey and how I feel about the choices I made that have led me to be an educator at Lewis University.

I grew up in the small Palestinian town of Bethlehem, a place characterized by violence and adversity, mainly due to the political instability and the Israeli military occupation of my region. During my childhood, I witnessed obscene events of killing and torture. Military tanks and sophisticated war machinery had become regular scenery in the small streets of my town. Additionally, the occupation resulted in imposing multiple military checkpoints, some of which I had to go through on a daily basis on my way to school. Oftentimes during these checkpoints, we would get treated inhumanely: I have seen people get beaten, spat on, and stripped to their underwear. Military curfews caused daily life to shut down on multiple occasions. Twice in the middle of the night, soldiers stormed into our house for no valid reason. The scariest moment in my memory from those days is the time that the soldiers occupying the building across from us started shooting randomly towards us as we sheltered inside our house, thinking we were protected there. Luckily, no one was physically hurt, although one of the bullets missed my mom by only a few inches. These events and this environment affected me immensely as a child. I developed a lot of insecurities, anxiety, and emotional vulnerability, causing me to have issues trusting others and oftentimes leading me to have doubts about myself and my ability to succeed in life. At the same time, these experiences fueled my curiosity about life, human actions, and "the other." From a young age, I remember asking a lot of questions: "How can humans be so cruel?" "Where is God in all this war and destruction?" "Are we—i.e., humans— inherently different?"

Growing up, my parents pushed my four siblings and me to take our education seriously; both had been teachers, rather strict ones, and they always wanted us to do well in school. They both had modest upbringings and humble beginnings. They worked hard to provide for us and offer us better lives. I learned much of my work ethic from them, and I look up to them. Their guidance during the early formative years of my life was essential in instilling a sense of becoming and direction. Primarily through my Catholic education and upbringing, my parents taught me to respect and care for all people; they made sure that I became engaged in various activities serving my community through scouts, voluntary work, church, and the local Christian youth organizations.

However, when I graduated high school, I felt that I wanted to take control of my life away from the influence of my parents, society, and expectations. I felt the need to assert some sort of personal identity. Against cultural norms, expectations, and the desires of my parents, I decided that I did not want to go to college right away, and I took a gap period in which I worked for a few months, traveled to Greece where I started studying Greek, and gave myself time to think about the next stage of my life. My thoughts at that time never provided a complete view of what my future would look like. However, I knew I wanted to pursue my studies in a business-related field. After researching various business disciplines, I decided to major in accounting because

I liked its systematic approach and the prospective career opportunities. Therefore, I enrolled at Bethlehem University, a Catholic Lasallian university in Palestine serving students from different religious and cultural backgrounds and known for its strong accounting program.

Bethlehem University provided me with safety, respect, and room for my inquisitiveness, which to me, and to many others, felt like a much-needed environment, not only because of the harsh conditions imposed by the military occupation, but also for the delicate social structure in my community. Bethlehem University, with its Lasallian mission, provided an atmosphere of diversity through education, dialogue, interfaith initiatives, and different university-required courses aimed at fostering intellectual growth and commitment to service. This atmosphere allowed me to get involved in diverse and vibrant settings where I met students from different backgrounds and faith traditions.

I found myself working with people completely different from myself in terms of their backgrounds and beliefs. Oftentimes, we would work on class projects and on-campus activities requiring us to ask each other difficult questions about our way of life and to admit to our misconceptions about them. Here I recall my experience with a particular friend whom I first met while working on a class project. He came to Bethlehem from a predominantly conservative Muslim city nearby. I was raised Catholic in Bethlehem, a city with Christian and Muslim populations. Growing up as a Christian minority, a lot of my activities involved the surrounding Christian population. I attended Christian schools, and I was mostly involved with Christian organizations and activities. Both my friend and I grew up in our own environments with minimal exposure to the larger community. Give our own insularity and cultural presumptions, we were not comfortable talking about our faiths and expressing our beliefs, and I expected our relationship to be contentious; we would not be compatible as friends because of our different religious upbringings, fearing we would judge and criticize each other and be self-righteous. However, we respected each other and wanted to work together on the project, and gradually with more conversation and discourse, we got closer to each other and started to be more involved in both of our social events. This has helped me to appreciate people who are different from me and further pushed me to be more comfortable seeking friendships with people who are different from me.

With such experiences, I learned how to open up to new possibilities and learn more about myself. As a young adult trying to make sense of the violence and injustices that surrounded my environment, I was profoundly influenced by the Lasallian experience that I had at Bethlehem University. It pushed me to define my priorities, and it is in that place where many of my perceptions have been molded. While at college and amidst my journey of personal and spiritual quest, I learned to listen more, observe more, reflect more, and care more.

I attribute my new perceptions and priorities to my encounters with the Christian Brothers and my frequent conversations with them. The Brothers were forthright, honest, and caring. During my sophomore year, I became close to Brother Peter Iorlano, one of the Brothers whose guidance has been instrumental in my life. I used to see him on campus walking around talking to students. I observed this from a distance, until one day, I was sitting on the bench in the courtyard, and he came towards me, and we started to converse. It was a casual conversation, but what I clearly remember is his delightful presence, the way he made me feel comfortable, and how smooth the conversation went. This incident was the opening for many conversations, and over time, I found myself approaching him whenever I needed advice or sought an answer about life, God, or religion. Even after all these years, we are still in contact with each other, and I connect with him and seek his guidance to this day. These encounters with him have taught me that I can trust in people and that it is okay to let go of some of my need to control and allow intervention in my life.

During my studies at Bethlehem, I was one of the few "unofficial" tutors for accounting. At that time, the University did not have an official tutoring program, so students would approach a few others who appeared to be diligent. Luckily, I was one of them. Being able to interact with my classmates and provide help filled me with joy and excitement. The tutoring experience helped me overcome some of my insecurities, build confidence, and explore ways to contribute. Furthermore, my appreciation for the educational setting at Bethlehem University and living with and through its mission made me realize the pivotal role of higher education in shaping lives, events, and progress in societies around the world. Looking back, I feel that this was the beginning of my journey to be a teacher. However, at that time, it was not clear to me that this is what I wanted or that I would end up doing. Gradually, however, it started to become more obvious that I wanted to be part of that mission and contribute to it.

After my graduation from Bethlehem University, I worked as an accountant but wanted to pursue graduate studies to fulfill my aspirations to be a teacher. After working for two years, I received the thrilling news that I was offered a scholarship to pursue my graduate studies at Lewis University. The scholarship program is a partnership between Lewis University and Bethlehem University, sponsored by the Christian Brothers and initiated by Brother James Gaffney, FSC. The program offers students the opportunity to pursue their graduate studies at Lewis and then return to teach at Bethlehem. I felt very privileged to receive such a unique opportunity, and it proved to be instrumental in developing my identity as a Lasallian educator.

I first arrived at Lewis in fall 2013. I did not know what to expect, and despite my excitement, I was apprehensive at first. I was coming to this new place where nothing was familiar and where I knew no one. I felt uneasy. This new setting was so much different from what I was used to, and I anticipated how difficult it would be to connect with others. However, the friendly environment at Lewis helped me feel accepted and welcomed. Many of the students, faculty, staff, and Christian Brothers were friendly and forthcoming. Whether it was other students in the dorm or cafeteria inviting me to join them for meals, faculty members being kind and caring, or Christian Brothers being supportive and thoughtful, all caused my apprehension to quickly dissipate.

The experience I had at Lewis University has further confirmed in my mind the appeal of the universal Lasallian values that I have learned and acquired in Bethlehem. My interactions and connections with the Christian Brothers had blissfully continued with the Brothers at Lewis, where I was constantly invited for socials and events. As international students, we were regularly cared for by the Brothers' community and often invited for holiday meals and gatherings. The Brothers would also celebrate our birthdays and special occasions. I felt fortunate to be close to them, to be able to have conversations and approach them for advice.

The Brothers' identity and their ethos of the Lasallian education greatly influenced me and continued to shape my identity. To see students and members of the faculty, staff, and the Christian Brothers enthusiastically play a dynamic part of campus life encouraged me to seek opportunities to be more active and involved. I joined University Ministry in a few volunteer activities; participated in a few panels and events representing my country and bringing awareness about the injustices and suffering in my region; and took on opportunities to help other international students get adjusted to life at Lewis. Actively participating in this environment highlighted for me the capacity of the Lasallian education at Lewis University to reflect on events and issues from the community and around the world.

In my studies for my master's in business administration degree, I learned much about business, economics, and the financial world. Classes discussed the role of business in the world and its powerful ability to affect lives. Business has been the catalyst for the greater good, but also, at times, tragic consequences. This dissonance and interplay between the powers of good and evil in the business world is a constant challenge. Throughout my education at Lewis, we discussed such issues with great emphasis on business ethics and corporate social responsibility. Knowing that I was going to be teaching similar topics after I graduated, I reflected on those issues and realized the ethical and mission-fulfilling role a business educator has. After spending two years studying for my graduate degree at Lewis University, my desire and preparedness to be involved in Lasallian education grew.

Upon my graduation from Lewis, I returned to Bethlehem University and taught in the accounting department for three years. During those formative years, I received critical mentorship from colleagues and the Christian Brothers. Fortunately, I was able to return to the United States and was invited to become a faculty member for Lewis University's College of Business. As a faculty member, I am always reminded of the powerful platform that I have and, therefore, the great responsibility I have towards our students. I have a responsibility not only to engage my students in discourse related to their academic studies, but also to associate with them, counsel and care for them, listen and learn from them, help them grow and realize their own potential. Whenever I feel discouraged, I use their diligence and perseverance as an inspiration, which helps me to move on and fulfill my vocation. This is where I am pushed to be the best version of myself, through demonstrating academic rigor, creating connections, and fostering interactions. I am a proud Lasallian who is committed to the Lasallian identity, trying my best to fortify its values in my approach to education and life wherever I go and in whatever position I am in.

One Step at a Time: The Way that Leads Me On

by Brother Larry Schatz, FSC

Director of Vocation Ministry for Lasalle Christian Brothers Midwest District
Member of the Lewis University Board of Trustees

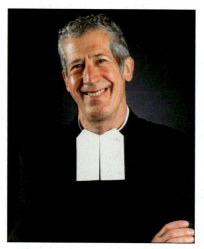

Every few years, I come upon a simple statement that grabs me and won't let me go. For example, a number of years ago at a gathering for young men thinking about being Brothers, one of the Brothers who presented said this: "Brotherhood is my path to God." And bam! There it was—the perfect summation of all that I believed about my vocation as a De La Salle Christian Brother. For me, the road that I'm traveling to—and with—God only makes sense in the context of brotherhood. And more specifically, as a follower of St. John Baptist de La Salle.

I've been a Brother for over forty years, but one of the most memorable experiences of brotherhood happened in 2015. That's when a group of Brothers from the United States joined with a group of Brothers from Spain to walk part of the Camino de Santiago de Compostela as a way of celebrating the Year of Consecrated Life. Better known simply as "The Camino," this ancient pilgrimage route in northern Spain has received renewed interest, thanks in part to the 2010 movie, "The Way." The Camino has proven to be a powerful experience for those who choose to walk either part of it or all of it. When I eagerly signed on to this fraternal adventure, I wasn't sure what to expect, but I knew that the Brothers from Spain have walked the Camino many times, so we American Brothers would be spared much of the detailed planning that goes with it. The only exception—and it's a big one—is that we had to pack for this overseas adventure. So, what do we need to bring with us? It was July, so we obviously didn't need a lot of layers. The big issue that we were all trying to figure out is what size backpack we should get. After plenty of research, a few of us decided on the same big bag: top of the line with solid back support, lots of pockets and flaps, and all the latest "backpack technology." And of course, in typical American style, we filled it, which meant that we overpacked. This became very clear when we met the Spanish Brothers and saw their small and simple backpacks. Lesson #1.

Our first day on the Camino, we set off with a lot of energy, but that quickly dissipated when we had to start climbing hills with our super-deluxe backpacks filled with "stuff." We managed to survive that first grueling day, but the burden we had placed on our backs, well, that was all on us. We had to live with it.

That first day, I learned another lesson. Every day, a group would wake up early to make coffee, but apparently Brother George and I did not get up early enough to get some. So after a couple of miles, we came upon a little restaurant, and we each ordered a cup of coffee to go. Well, guess what? We were told that they don't have coffee to go. Seriously? However, we were invited to have a seat outside, and it would be brought to us. And so it was, and we both realized how good it felt to park for a bit and truly savor the coffee and ambience. Lesson #2.

A little further on came lesson #3. The Camino trail is quite well-marked. Whenever there was a fork in the road or multiple paths before us, we only had to look for the stone marker decorated with a seashell and a yellow arrow, and we would continue on the route—sort of like the yellow brick road, but more subtle. Simple enough, right? Except a few of us caught up in a lively conversation missed a route marker. It was only after fifteen or twenty minutes, as we came upon an intersection with no marker in sight, that we realized that we had not seen an arrow for quite some time. Uh-oh. Now what? Well, the only solution was the obvious one: We had to reverse direction and watch for a Camino sign. We eventually found one, but that took us around forty-five minutes of needless walking.

So, the three lessons I learned on that first—and toughest—day are these: #1: Pack light. Just take what you really need. #2: Slow down, take a break, unburden yourself for a bit, and savor the moment (along with the coffee). And #3: Pay attention! There are signs and markers, but it's easy to miss them.

These also serve as great lessons for the journey of life that we are all on:

1. What do we *really* need on life's journey? What baggage do we bring with us that is weighing us down?

2. What's the rush? Take time to be in the moment, to breathe and relax a bit. The path is always there. And we can get back on it with renewed energy and zeal.

3. What do we need to pay attention to? Notice where you are and see what—and who—is around you. Don't miss the signposts that God sends our way. It's so easy to miss all kinds of opportunities and sights when we're preoccupied and distracted.

The Camino has lots of lessons to share, and its impact on me has lasted. I resolved to do it again, and so I did, four years later, this time with three friends. We took a different Camino route, and this time, we had to figure out the logistics ourselves. And yes, I did pack lighter!

Walking the many varieties of paths that are part of the Camino felt familiar to me. I grew up in western North Dakota, and our family home was at the end of a graveled road. I spent much of my boyhood playing on that road and the other dirt roads and paths around our home and in our rural neighborhood. In my imagination, they often became trails, leading to a new adventure. A fond memory comes from summers many years later when, as adults, my two sisters and I had moved far away from where we grew up. We'd return home, usually around the Fourth of July, and the three of us would get up early and walk all those familiar dirt roads around our place. It was so good to have that bonding time, just the three of us. Plus, there's something about walking that encourages conversation. And because so much of the Camino involves dirt paths, I felt right at home as I pursued yet another adventure on the Camino trail.

Through my many adventures and encounters on my two Caminos, one thing is clear: The Camino is now very much part of my life and spirituality. I plan to return again, and this time I hope to accompany a group of young people. I can't think of a better way to concretize what a faith journey is all about—or better put—a pilgrimage. And that word—"pilgrimage"—is key to both the Camino and our life journey. There's a big difference between being a tourist and being a pilgrim. Many of us have been tourists, and that's a good thing, but tourist and pilgrim are most definitely not synonyms. For tourists, days usually consist of stopping at famous sites, taking photos, and learning more about a culture—in other words, to be an observer. That said, I don't think any of us want to be tourists on this journey of life, do we? For pilgrims, it is much more intentional. It is not about sightseeing, even though there's plenty to see. Rather, it's about walking the road and being open to what each day brings. In fact, while walking the Camino, you are considered a "peregrino" (Spanish for pilgrim), and when fellow pilgrims meet on the path or at a stop, they will greet one another with "Buen Camino." That's not easy to translate into English because of the richness of the word Camino and all that it implies.

And so, here's another thing about the Camino that serves as a metaphor for life. In both my experiences, we would all agree on our daily destination, so we knew that we would reunite there at some point. Typically, each of us would start the day in the company of others, because usually we'd all head out at the same time. Inevitably, however, you'd end up walking with one other person, then for a while by yourself, and then often with other pilgrims from around the world. Naturally, the Camino allows for lots of time to reflect and think. For me, that meant praying, which is simply walking with God and sharing what's going on within me and around me. And even if I felt like I could not take one more step, I just kept going, fueled by both the desire to "get there" as well as the anticipation of being

> **"** For tourists, days usually consist of stopping at famous sites, taking photos, and learning more about a culture—in other words, to be an observer. That said, I don't think any of us want to be tourists on this journey of life, do we? **"**

together to share a meal and some excellent Spanish wine.

At the end of each day, we would come together and share our experiences while on the road. What did we see? Who did we meet? What surprised us? What struggles did we have? A daily rhythm developed that can become a roadmap for every day of our life. And sharing each day's highlights and challenges helped us capture the blessings of that day. I find now that I cannot end my day without reflecting, journaling, and focusing on what I have learned and am grateful for, and for me, that leads naturally into prayer.

We've all heard the saying: "It's the journey, not the destination." In the case of the Camino—and life—it's actually both. Arriving at the sumptuous Cathedral of Santiago de Compostela is an exhilarating event, one that often involves tears of joy. But again, isn't that an apt metaphor for our life's journey? Where are we headed? To be a pilgrim is to be on The Way. But to where? And what or who is waiting for us at our journey's end?

On the Camino, we eventually arrive at a holy place, and there we are with our fellow pilgrims, coming at last to where the path has led us. Yes, our feet are sore, and we're tired of wearing the same thing every day, and really tired of lugging around our gigantic backpacks. But what is so wonderful is that all of us there in that spacious plaza have come from so many different places, both geographically and spiritually. And more than not, through it all, we were praying with our feet. No matter how worn out you felt, you knew deep inside that you were called to this, to this winding road with your fellow pilgrims. And so, step by aching step, you just kept going. And you're never really alone on that path.

Because brotherhood is my path to God, my response to my vocational call, I feel so fortunate and blessed to have shared my first Camino with my fellow Brothers. Besides the familiar greeting of "Buen Camino," there is another term that pilgrims would often say to encourage one another: "Ultreia!" No one is quite sure of the origin of that term, but I like to translate it as "Ever onward!" So many times, just a smile or a word of encouragement can make all the difference in our—or someone else's—day. And one more thing: It's really not so much about which path we take, but more about how intentionally and attentively we walk along that path. Yes, we're going to stumble, we'll get tired, and no doubt we'll miss a few signposts along the way, but through it all, we are given companions for our journey, and God is right there with us.

My life as a Brother has been filled with blessings and adventures, but the Camino remains a pivotal experience. Being on "The Way"—being attentive and reflective as we walk the path before us—serves as a reminder that a journey implies movement and a direction. And just when you think that you can't walk another step, you'll hear a "Buen Camino," or come upon a little cafe, and your body and spirit are revived. Grace happens. And the road ahead keeps beckoning. And the journey goes on.

Thou my source,
and my returning,
my beginning
and welcome home,
bless the path
on which I journey;
be the way
that leads me on.
—*Jan Richardson*

Finding Life-Giving Work

by Laura Wilmarth Tyna, M.A.

Director of Community Engaged Learning

As a child, I spent time each summer visiting my grandparents. They lived on a farm in North Central Illinois, and I loved waking up and sitting in their kitchen, waiting for my Grandpa Gene to return from doing chores in the early hours of the day.

He would come back into the house smelling of sweat and hay, overalls hooked over one shoulder while the other clasp swung by his side, and a baseball cap covering his last few strands of hair. He refused to wear a shirt in the summer, so his skin was a honey brown color, and his chest hair would be dusty, having trapped flecks of hay while he fed the cows. Grandpa would ask gruffly, "Are you sitting in my chair?" while I giggled with delight. This was *our* time. The time of day when my Grandma Judy slept in, and I got Grandpa, in all his pretend grumpiness, to myself over a bowl of cereal.

The days with my grandparents were filled with adventures with cousins, aunts, and uncles who lived nearby. My dad's family—which included eight living children, their spouses, and children—was my first community. Playing with some of my twenty-three first cousins taught me a lot about handling conflict with civility! And in between swimming at the neighbor's pool and exploring the barn for kittens or enjoying cookouts with farm-fresh steak and sweet corn, my grandma and grandpa exposed me to what it means to work for the common good, as we spent some time every summer at the local food pantry. "People Helping People," the official name of the pantry, was a resource for community members who were struggling financially to cover the costs of food, clothes, or even their rent or mortgage that month. I didn't realize it then, but Grandma Judy ran the organization in her town of 2,500 people, in addition to working year-round with the local Salvation Army.

Back then, my grandma was a short, round woman with curly, dark brown hair, pale skin, a friendly smile, and a passion for helping others. Where my grandpa was skilled at making people laugh and feel good—think belly-laughing toddlers and knee-smacking adults—my grandma was gifted at going out of her way to let others know that they weren't alone. It's clear to me now that I've always held them as the gold standard for what it looks like to invite others into connection.

I loved going with Grandma to People Helping People. I'd help distribute food, lay out donated clothes and toys, or play with kids who came in with their parents. At the time, I thought it was fun to be a helper, and I felt very important contributing to something bigger than myself, something that I wasn't often invited to do as a kid, the baby, at home. I also really enjoyed meeting people and having conversations with them. I saw my grandma welcome each person into the pantry, and sometimes into her own kitchen, with love, kindness, and openness. She didn't judge people for seeking out help. Instead, she respected and honored the dignity of each person, doing whatever she could to help them through their circumstances.

Looking back, I can clearly make the connection between those summer visits with my grandparents and my chosen career in community engagement—a type of learning which takes students into the local community to learn more deeply about a course topic—but I couldn't have guessed it then. Perhaps more important to note, I wouldn't be exposed to a career even remotely like the one I selected for nearly ten years, as I concluded my college experience!

As my life progressed from those days on the farm, I took on leadership roles that allowed me to do the work of building community. I participated in activities that I enjoyed: student council, dance team, and a peer helpers' program that provided training for how to support other students, during high school; assisting with orientation, the counseling center, and an intergroup dialogue program, in college. Through these experiences, I learned about interacting with my peers and other adults as I participated in small communities. I learned about who I am, and the social justice issues related to a person's identity, and I realized that I'm passionate about justice issues and creating inclusive communities.

One such moment of learning in college occurred as part of the intergroup dialogue program in which I participated. This initiative engaged students from different backgrounds (i.e., People of Color and White people, Christians and Jews, Latinos and African Americans) in constructive conversation about difference. Through this initiative, I had a chance to explore my own identity and to engage with others around issues such as race, social class, religious diversity, and sexual orientation. This was an excellent way to learn about community because we explored the issues that often divide us from each other and keep us from being in authentic relationships.

The instructors for this three-semester program were two amazing women who served as mentors and guides. Lydia was a warm, funny psychologist of Palestinian descent who was in a same-sex relationship. She was the first openly gay person with whom I had a real relationship. Joycelyn was a fair-skinned African American woman with a big personality. She was smart, passionate, and a bit intimidating to me because she wasn't afraid to share her opinion ... something that felt super scary to me as a nineteen-year-old, White woman talking about race for the first time. I will always remember the day that Joycelyn challenged my notion of community and helped me to recognize that being in connection means being real—even when it is difficult or challenges someone else's ideas about truth.

During that time, a man was moving around my campus community shooting people, seemingly at random. A Jewish man had been shot and injured, and a few other folks had just missed being hit. In the early 2000s, shootings were far less common than they are today, but they were just as terrifying. The entire campus was on edge, and a lot of folks questioned their safety, as they wondered if the shooter was targeting people based on identity—the first man was Jewish, other potential victims were people of color.

In my intergroup relations course, we discussed our feelings about the shooting with Joycelyn and Lydia. When I shared that I didn't really know too much about what was happening, Joycelyn looked at me for a moment, and then said, "Your response makes me so angry! This is exactly what privilege looks like. Because you are not a person who feels like their identity is a risk, you haven't even paid attention to what's happening. People around you are terrified, and you have no idea what's happening!"

To say that I felt embarrassed and ashamed would be an understatement. I wanted to crawl under the desk and hide. And the worst part was that I knew she was right. I was able to neglect what was happening around me because I didn't think it applied to me, even though people I cared about—like Joycelyn—were scared for their lives. I was mortified and wished that I'd never have to see Joycelyn again. But that's the thing about community—when you're part of something bigger than yourself, you're connected to each other whether you like it or not. This was a pivotal moment for me in understanding community. It helped me recognize that being in a diverse community—with differences in age, race, religion, sexual orientation, experience, and thought—created a space where honest dialogue can lead to personal growth. This was an important revelation for me, though I still didn't have any idea of how these lessons about community would relate to my future career.

As my senior year of college began, I had an "aha" moment: All the activities I loved were coordinated out of the Student Services building. And that building was filled with people who had jobs! I had never considered looking at my advisors, supervisors, and mentors as people with jobs that I might explore for my own future career. It was then that I started to look into careers in higher education and student affairs.

Today, as the Director of Community Engaged Learning at Lewis University, I can draw dotted lines to the moments when I connected to the values that have guided my career. Being in **community** with my extended family, food pantry-goers, and many of the folks I met in high school or college, helped me to understand that we all need to rely upon each other. We "do life" best when we're doing it in mutually respectful **connection** with one-another! Learning about injustice and the exclusion of others who are seen as different due to race, sexual orientation, religion, or some other characteristic of identity helped me to understand the essential nature of **creating inclusive communities**. The moment with Joycelyn really helped me understand that point.

My role at Lewis is focused on developing partnerships through which students can learn by engaging in the community. I support faculty members in creating opportunities to learn about a topic through *doing* related work. For example, I could help a faculty member find non-profit organizations with which their students can create and begin to implement a strategic marketing plan. Or, I may coordinate a group of students to tutor youth every week at a nearby community center. This might sound complicated, but I find that it's really about being *with* people, listening, and empathizing. I listen to faculty members, trying to understand what their students are learning and what skills those students have to offer. I listen to non-profit professionals to hear about their organizations' priorities and goals and explore how students might support those efforts. My work allows me to engage students in community to build relationships and contribute in meaningful ways. It's truly all about those core values that my family and experiences helped me to develop as a child and young adult. My growing-up years absolutely prepared me for this work!

I did not understand along the way exactly what my future path would be. I hadn't figured it out early on: I was not one of those kids who knew what they wanted to do by the time they were twelve! I wasn't even aware that a career in higher education was a thing. However, along the way, I took advantage of opportunities to participate in ways that I enjoyed, and I listened to my moral compass—those values that have guided me throughout the years. I also sought out people who were willing to mentor me, who challenged me to think about how I wanted to show up in the world when I wasn't sure what came next or what the right decision was. By seeking out this support and affirmation, I found a career—a calling—which feeds my soul. It gives meaning to my life in many ways and makes coming to work fulfilling and life-giving.

Ride the Headwinds

by Megan Zahos, M.B.A., M.S.

Class of '06 and '12
Associate Professor and Associate Director of Aviation Flight (Formerly Employed)

Here we are at last. The beginning of what's next. Our resolve, tenacity, perseverance, and strength have driven us here. Recently, life has probably seemed like an acceleration of decisions. A checklist of important tasks to achieve to reach our destinations. A race of applications, packing, and goodbyes. Box up our treasures, *check.* Give the dog one last treat, *check.* Move into the dorms, *check.* Tell Mom not to cry as she's driving home, *check.* Try not to scare your roommate on the first day, *check.* And now, checklist complete. For a moment, we're finished and still.

This pause in momentum may be disorienting. To be at the beginning again is surprisingly unfamiliar. There's a new checklist with a daunting number of unchecked boxes. And although every unchecked box holds the promise of possibility and opportunity, rebuilding the momentum that brought us here will take focus and determination. But as Henry Ford once said, "When everything seems to be going against you, remember that the airplane takes off against the wind, not with it." And even though beginnings can be a battlefield of certainty and doubt, life's greatest journeys are filled with headwinds. As we stand in the doorway of your next adventure, ready to turn into the wind once more, I'd like to share some of the experiences that inspired me to ride the headwinds.

Many of our hopes and dreams are rooted in an experience that we had as children. A special moment or inspiring event that ignites a spark, an idea, and then a purpose. A future you starts to take shape. A first beginning.

My first beginning wasn't easy. I was born somewhere in Missouri, surrounded by strangers, to people I've never met. The folks that created me faced some headwinds of their own and, upon my birth, surrendered me to the good people of the Missouri Department of Social Services, where I entered foster care. Fortunately for me, Moms and Dads can come into people's lives in many different ways. Some are there from birth; others pick you up a little later in life. I remember my parents telling me the story of my beginning, and I was more than a little indignant about my circumstances. I thought of myself as quite a catch. How could someone just give me away? And now, as I faced my first headwind, doubt chipped away at my certainty. They noticed my distress and reminded me, "Superman was adopted." This did improve my mood. After all, I had just learned that I was basically Superman. My parents regretted this conversation when I tried to test my ability to fly by jumping off most everything. This was the spark.

Now, how to fly .... The jumping isn't working. I'll have to pick a more traditional career path than Superman. And just like that, airplanes entered my life. Pilot. That should get the job done. The spark had blossomed into something more—an idea. The future me was starting to come together.

I faced my next headwind in an airport. We were traveling to visit relatives for the holidays and preparing to board our flight. There I stood, nose pressed against the smooth glass of the terminal window. Outside sat an airplane. My dad pretended he hadn't already asked the captain if I could sit in the cockpit, thinking to surprise me. But I knew he had worked his Dad magic. He worked for the airline and seemed to know everyone. I could barely stand still, trying to contain myself so I wouldn't ruin the surprise and miss the twinkle in his eyes when he finally decided to let me in on the secret. The captain strode towards us with his uniform—his stripes and his invisible cape—and opened the door to the jetway.

We walked down the corridor, cool from the winter air, to the smells of jet fuel mixed with snow, the perfect smell to a kid with dreams of Christmas and airplanes.

Finally, the cockpit. The huge captain's seat. The endless rows of important switches that I wanted so badly to touch. He showed me everything, and I showed him everything, both excitedly talking at once, united by the specialness of the moment. My dad was bursting with pride, standing a little straighter every time I pointed to something he had taught me. "Someday," I say, "I'll be pushing those buttons." Then, the captain kneels next to me, and I lean in, waiting for the wisdom I knew he would impart, the words that would guide me to my dream. With a puzzled tone, he asks, "Wouldn't you rather be a flight attendant, sweetie?"

I never noticed that there weren't any women. I remember hearing his words and pulling my hand back abruptly as if I had touched a hot stove. *You're not supposed to be here.* As I scrambled to remove myself from this sacred place, I could feel the cape sliding off my shoulders. *I'm no Superman.*

This wasn't the only time I would lose my cape. Doubt is a traitorous thing. It conspires against us and destroys our momentum, like brakes grinding us to a halt. It tricks us into thinking our accomplishments are the result of serendipity rather than resolve. Obstacles to our aspirations feel like evidence, corroboration, and proof that our doubts are well-founded. The truth I learned on this day: Obstacles don't block the path—they *are* the path. You have to climb over them.

My next big headwind came later in life. I had just begun my senior year in college at the University of Illinois. I successfully navigated my way through three years of flight training and was working as a part-time flight instructor with students of my own while I finished earning my undergraduate degree. Every day was an exciting new adventure, and the future was bright. I had positioned myself to graduate with the flight time required to move on to an airline, joined student organizations to make connections and gain leadership experience, earned good grades, and built a résumé that would make me competitive. *I can't wait to push all those buttons.* The date was September 11th, 2001. I remember turning on the television news as I got ready for my first class of the day. They were reporting that a small airplane had hit the World Trade Center. I could see smoke coming out of the building and bright blue skies. Not a cloud in sight. That doesn't make any sense at all …. Then I watched the second plane hit live. *That wasn't a small plane. That wasn't an accident.* Next came the Pentagon, then collapse of the south tower, Flight 93 in Pennsylvania, finally the collapse of the north tower, and fearfully waiting for more. *What am I watching? How many people did I just see die? The national airspace system is closed. What does that even mean?* I called the airport. I was supposed to fly later. *Can I still fly? What's happening?* Everybody was told

to land wherever they were. Students were stranded at other airports. Commercial flights headed to Chicago were directed to land in Champaign and were crowding our ramp. I looked up and realized there's no one there. Silence, emptiness, no one in the skies. *What. Is. Happening?* Suddenly, I heard another flight instructor say, "No one is going to want to fly after this." And while we watched the world crumble, we wondered if we were watching our futures crumble with it.

That day was devastating for the airline industry. Jobs were lost, all hiring stopped, and airlines went out of business. One of them was the airline my dad worked for, Trans World Airlines. A legacy carrier, the airline I grew up on, the company I thought that I'd spend my life and career with—gone. It's difficult to describe how unmoored I felt during the days and months that followed. The checklist I had so carefully used to check all the right boxes now seemed pointless. I was lost. Then one day, I saw one of my students visibly upset. I quietly approached and asked him if he was okay. He was a freshman, just starting his flight training, and he was feeling much the same as I was—scared for the future, directionless, and filled with doubt. I realized that it wasn't just we seniors that were lost. I wanted to help him but didn't know how. In the past, flight instructing had been a technical event for me. The subject matter is complex, learning how to operate the aircraft is challenging, and the testing process is rigid and demanding. Seeing the doubt on that student's face, seeing it fill his soul, changed everything. I could see his cape sliding to the floor. Suddenly I felt direction again, a new checklist. The world might be crazy, but this kid's flight training doesn't have to be. Finally, the spark that became an idea evolved into a purpose. Teaching.

As we soldiered on through the rest of the school year, enduring the uncertainty of the time, graduation came. This day is usually something that students look forward to, but we approached the date with trepidation, unsure of what the future held for us. Our commencement address was given by the great Maya Angelou. One of the things she said was, "Light someone's path." It was an inspirational speech for a group of people desperate for an inspiration.

From that point forward, my teaching style evolved. It transformed into something that went beyond technical knowledge. I made the decision to move from delivering information to creating wisdom. It was the difference between teaching someone how to become literate and opening their minds to the joys of literature; the difference between teaching them notes on a piano and showing them how to compose a symphony. I realized the impact of my words, the influence of my actions. I could not just teach the technical but must create a confidence that is necessary to keep capes firmly in place on the shoulders of my students. This revelation, these headwinds, changed the direction of my life, and I've endeavored to be the light in someone's path ever since.

Now here we stand, at the beginning of what's next, having encountered one of the strongest headwinds any of us have seen in years. A generation struggling to fight against losing itself in the doubt created by the upheaval of COVID-19, its continuing effects, and other gales affecting our world. As we look back on what we may have lost, try to remember what we have gained. Our headwinds have taught us resiliency, adaptability, and persistence in the face of the impossible. They helped us develop the ability to overcome. We have faced challenges that the world hasn't faced in a century, and yet here we stand, checklist in hand, ready to take off into the wind once more, eager to see what our next beginning will bring. As our sparks blossom into purpose, we climb over any obstacles in the way. With our capes firmly in place, we face our next headwind with confidence. As E. E. Cummings said, "It takes courage to grow up and become who you really are."

Sometimes the Call is Literally a Call

by Mike Zegadlo, M.A.

Class of '96 and '02
Chief of Police

Being police chief at Lewis University is the toughest job I've ever had. And that's coming from a guy who used to make a living breaking up bar fights, responding to violent domestic incidents, and arresting intoxicated motorists. Sure, those things cause momentary situational stress, but I'd rather wrestle a drunk in the street any night than try to figure how I'm going to keep gas in the police cars when the fuel budget is in the red or pour over the annual crime report to avoid a fifty-thousand-dollar federal fine because of errant math. That's the kind of stress that keeps me up at night. This job isn't fun, and that's okay because this job is exactly the job I'm meant to be doing at this moment in my life.

There is no reference to fun in most definitions of vocation because vocation is not about self-gratification. It's about figuring out where one's talents intersect with a greater community need. It's about listening to a calling, which sometimes speaks subtly but at other times is infinitely more apparent, and then having the courage to run headlong in that direction even if you know the road ahead won't be easy. Don't get me wrong. I'm not claiming to be courageous. I'm a simple guy, not an intellectual or a philosopher, just a traveler trying to navigate a journey. God knows this about me, which is why my "call" to service has more than once been a literal "call" from a person in my life, someone I know and trust well enough to believe that the call may be a communiqué from a much higher authority. My responses to those calls have led me to critical crossroads on my vocational path, even when I'm not entirely sure how or why it all works. Parker Palmer, in *Let Your Life Speak* (2000), explains this phenomenon as "something I can't not do, for reasons I'm unable to explain to anyone else and don't fully understand myself but that are nonetheless compelling" (25).

> ❝
>
> To stay in that role—that would have been too easy, because vocation is not about what's fun. It's about what's meaningful, and what makes an impact, and where your talents serve a need.
>
> ❞

My own attempt to understand how I got here requires me to reflect on numerous variables in my personal evolutionary equation, beginning with my natural gifts. I'm good at only three things: I run fast. Well, at least I did twenty years and twenty pounds ago. I shoot straight, both literally with a handgun and in my interpersonal communication. And finally, I'm a good teacher. That last one has been the guardrail on my career roadway.

There are things I desperately wanted to be good at, like music. After playing in a series of unsuccessful rock bands in high school and college, I finally had to come to the realization that, as much as I love music, and wanted to be the next Jon Bon Jovi, I didn't have that talent. As a kid, I fantasized about being an Air Force pilot, specifically an F-16 driver, like Doug Masters in the 1980s movie *Iron Eagle*, but I'm bad at math, so that was off the table.

Teaching, however, was something that brought me joy and for which I had some talent. Though my subject matter has changed considerably over the years, teaching has always been something I've known I'm meant to do. I figured this out about myself when I was a teenager. There was a formative, albeit traumatic, experience which helped to point me in the right direction.

As the senior patrol leader in Boy Scout Troop 406, it was my job to teach new Scouts the proper use of the axe in the axe yard. This was an important rite of passage for first-year Scouts. Successfully completing a structured training course, memorizing, and abiding by several safety rules, and demonstrating competence in handling a knife, wood tools, and the axe, entitled a Scout to be issued a "Totin' Chip" card. It was like a driver's license for sharp objects. Once in possession of the coveted Totin' Chip, a Scout could carry a pocketknife, use wood chisels to carve, and, with proper permission and supervision in a roped-off axe yard, cut firewood. I enjoyed instructing the course. It was my first teaching gig, and I took it very seriously.

Tad was my first "student" that hot, August morning. I gathered the half dozen or so new Scouts in our campsite's axe yard at the Owasippe Scout Reservation, nestled in the lush, green woods of Whitehall, Michigan. It was a five-hour drive from Troop 406's home parish on the Southwest Side of Chicago, but it felt like a world away. I'd given the required safety briefing, checked swing clearances, and verified all participants knew all the safety rules. I pointed to Tad to step forward to demonstrate his swing. As he entered the axe yard, I sized him up to verify he was in compliance with all required safety equipment which, most importantly, included boots. Tad's tan, faux-leather, kid-sized construction boots, which I imagined his mother found on the clearance rack at Venture or Zayre, were untied. Proud that I'd spotted the safety violation, I sternly directed Tad out of "my" axe yard until his boots were properly secured.

I instructed several other rookie Scouts, fresh out of their Webelos Dens, over the next half-hour without incident. Attention turned back to Tad, now the only Scout who had not proven his prowess with the axe. As Tad meandered into the axe yard again, I repeated my inspection. This time, I noticed his laces were pulled tightly, but still not tied. "Tad, what the hell?!" I blurted out in frustration. He turned around, exited the axe yard, and began to sob as he walked away. Tad was prone to crying, so this was nothing unusual. Tad's father, Ray, was an insufferable jerk who regularly publicly scolded Tad, frequently causing him to cry.

I followed Tad out of the axe yard, feeling guilty that I'd made him cry. I took him out of earshot of the other Scouts and asked why he hadn't tied his boots. His response was unexpected, "I can't." I asked for clarification, "What do you mean you can't?" This eleven-year-old Boy Scout then informed me that he had never been taught to tie his shoes.

I spent the next hour teaching a new subject matter: shoe tying. I taught Tad how to tie his shoes, and then how to swing an axe. That was a day I'll never forget for many reasons. My teaching made a real impact on Tad's quality of life. I had been able to fill a void Tad had in his development by taking some time his father didn't have or wouldn't give. Tad and I bonded that day. I knew he appreciated that I taught him to tie his shoes and to swing an axe, but more importantly, he appreciated that when we returned to the axe yard, I told no one that he didn't know how to tie his shoes. This seminal teaching experience was the start of my calling. But Tad's impact on my vocational journey wasn't over. The next impact would be more profound, and just two months later.

Tad's coffin was heavier than I expected it to be, even though there were five other uniformed Scouts helping me carry it. I felt like I had all the weight. I looked behind me to see six more Scout uniforms carrying the coffin of Tad's younger sister, Kim, and, behind her, six more carrying the coffin of his mother, Pat. Their murders were brutal, and the news that Tad's father had done it and then set the house on fire was almost more than I could handle.

I can play the afternoon of October 10, 1990, like a movie in my head. I remember walking up our concrete driveway—ours was one of only two houses on the block with a driveway. The grey, chain-link fence gate was secured by a latch that had to be lifted at a specific angle to keep it from binding on the aluminum post. I pushed the button on the back storm door, my book bag slung over my right shoulder. My mom met me on the stairs. I knew by her face she had bad news. "The Sojaks have been murdered. It was Ray." I stared back at her blankly. It did not cognitively register. "Our Sojaks?" I wondered. Maybe she meant a different family. Or maybe there were some other "Sojaks." My mom clarified this unimaginable reality to me. I turned back out the door, enraged. I flung the book bag into the air so high it almost hit the telephone line running from the back of the house to the alley. I screamed in a voice I didn't recognize. "I just taught that kid to tie his shoes. He didn't know how to tie his shoes, and I just taught him to tie his shoes." It seemed so futile. *Why had I even bothered teaching Tad to tie his shoes?* Tad had the ability to tie shoes for only two months.

Teaching Tad to tie his shoes was life-altering—an act of love between Tad and me. It momentarily filled a void left by his father. I was able to be a father to him for those few minutes. On one level, it affirmed my calling to teach, but this particular lesson was deeper. His murder filled me with rage directed at his father, a man who couldn't teach his kid to tie his shoes but didn't hesitate to murder him when the family finances collapsed. Someone should have been able to protect Tad. I felt helpless. I was scared and angry. I wanted to prevent that from ever happening to anyone like Tad again. That raw emotion got buried somewhere deep inside me, leaving a scar on my soul. At the age of seventeen, I was unequipped to process it. The rage, the desire to protect the weak and defeat the wicked, was put in a sealed container for later, when I had the emotional maturity to process it, to integrate it into a more developed mind. I focused on the more positive, heart-warming idea of being a teacher as a way to honor Tad. But that impulse to be a guardian, to protect Tad, never left me. It haunted me. It lingered and waited for a time when it could re-emerge and change my vocational journey in a dramatic way.

My first literal call came in August of 1996 from Brother Bob Murphy, a Carmelite who, at the time, was Lewis University's Director of Ministry. Having completed my undergraduate degree in history and Type 09 teaching certificate, I was subbing at Argo Community High School and waiting tables while interviewing for full-time teaching jobs. Br. Bob beeped my pager while I was working a shift at the now defunct Candlelight Dinner Playhouse, where I had recently been promoted from server to table captain. On break, I used my Tandy CT-350 cellular telephone stowed under the front seat of my 1986 Chevrolet Celebrity to return Br. Bob's call. He told me the Director of Residence Life at Lewis, Kathy Slattery, was in a bind. Her assistant director, who was supposed to have been planning resident assistant and hall director training, abruptly quit the day before training was to start. They needed someone who could step into the role immediately and hit the ground running. Br. Bob knew

I hadn't found a full-time job yet and given my previous experience at Lewis as a resident assistant and hall director, it might be a good match.

That "call" from Br. Bob changed my path from high school teacher to student affairs practitioner. Because I trusted Br. Bob, and he told me that this position was a good opportunity for me and for Lewis, I accepted the invitation. It was the beginning of what would be a ten-year run in student affairs, first at Lewis, then at North Central College where I served as an Assistant Dean of Students. I learned a new way to teach. Meeting students at critical moments in their journey, often in crisis or on the heels of some incident which put them at odds with campus policies, I found a new subject matter—student development. I flourished in this new career field and felt I'd found my calling. That is, until a new calling presented itself.

As part of my responsibilities at North Central, I supervised the director of campus safety, the college's security department. I knew nothing about law enforcement or public safety, and, not wanting to be an administrator in charge of a department about which I had no operational knowledge, I set out to educate myself and learn everything I could about it. The more I learned, the more intrigued I became. I was in my early thirties at the time, married and with a daughter. Something I cannot explain drew me toward the field of law enforcement. Maybe it was my family's history of military service. My dad, his brother, and my brother all served. I opted, instead, to pierce my ear, grow my hair, and carry a six-string instead of an M4. Maybe it was post-September 11th patriotism. Maybe those feelings I'd pushed deep down after Tad's death were creeping back up: that desire to protect Tad and defeat the villains that would do harm to the weak. "For reasons I'm unable to explain to anyone else and don't fully understand myself," as Palmer said (25), I left higher education and became a police officer with the City of Naperville. I started over completely, from the bottom, in a new career field, one in which I had no experience or expertise.

Being a municipal patrol cop was the most fun I ever had at a job. It was the first time in my career that I was not a boss. I was just "one of the guys." I had a team of brothers and sisters in arms. Together we faced our nightly adventures of responding to complex, often dangerous, problems which our community members could not or would not be able to solve on their own. It was a bond I had not previously experienced. The joy of sitting around the Dunkin' Donuts at 3:00 a.m. debriefing that "hot" call we just handled was something only those who've weathered trauma together can understand. It's an intimate camaraderie understood only by military, police, first responders, health care workers, and the like.

To stay in that role—that would have been too easy, because vocation is not about what's fun. It's about what's meaningful, and what makes an impact, and where your talents serve a need. All those elements were in place during my time at Naperville. I was doing good work, serving my community. But there was something better waiting. That's when the second literal "call" came. This time, Kathy Slattery, now the Dean of Student Services at Lewis, was trying to start a police department at the University to replace the existing security department. They had already hired and subsequently lost two directors who were to have transitioned the department from security to police. It turned out there was a big difference between law enforcement culture and higher education culture, and it was difficult for career cops to transition to being teachers of student development. What was needed was someone who had some experience in both student affairs and law enforcement. Kathy thought I might be the person. I didn't agree, but I trusted Kathy. This call was presenting me with an opportunity to return to Lewis again, this time in a much different capacity. It was a difficult choice to leave my comrades in arms at Naperville P.D., but this calling was too powerful to ignore. God was pointing me back to Lewis to do both things I'd learned to love and for which I had developed some level of competence. I was going to teach in a new environment, with new subject matter, in a new, more complex, and meaningful way.

Whether my subject matter is axe handling, U.S. history, student development, or combat pistol tactics for patrol officers, I am grateful for the opportunity to teach. I am grateful for the opportunity to participate in a vocation in which I can see the direct impact of my work. It's not perfect. I regularly make and learn from mistakes. I stumble as a leader and teacher. I occasionally long for the carefree life of an autonomous, midnight-shift patrol officer, responsible only for my own actions. An objective cost/benefit analysis of my decision to return to Lewis and leave municipal policing might yield an unfavorable result in terms of my retirement portfolio or adjusted gross income. But vocation isn't about income. It is not a concrete, black and white thing. It's intangible. It's soulful. In its purest form, it connects inexplicable impulses of a spiritual calling with the practical application of knowledge, skills, and abilities. The end product is a feeling of rightness which can't be substantiated with a pay stub or performance evaluation but, nonetheless, leaves the soul satisfied for having answered the call.

Works Cited

Palmer, Parker. *Let Your Life Speak: Listening for the Voice of Vocation*. San Francisco: Jossey-Bass, 2000.

Discussion Questions

The following questions can be applied to any of the stories included in the collection.

1) Which life stories did you most connect with or learn from? In what ways?

2) Based on one or more of the life stories:

   a. How would you define vocation or calling?

   b. What are some sources of, or pathways to, a vocation-calling?

   c. Which sources or pathways relate to your own path so far?

   d. What are some helpful practices for discerning a vocation-calling?

   e. Which discerning practices do you already use, or might you begin to use, to help you develop more self-awareness and further clarify a vocation-calling?

   f. What were some obstacles or detours that the authors experienced, and how were they navigated?

   g. What obstacles have you encountered in your life experiences, and how have you navigated them?

   h. What have you learned about yourself from any of your own challenging experiences that may help you discern a vocation-calling?

3) From the book's Introduction:

   a. How is vocation-calling a creative process?

   b. How is framing vocation-calling as a creative process helpful for the journey?

4) From *The Encounter* photo essay:

   a. In what ways do the story and illustrations of creating *The Encounter* reflect the creative process of a vocation-calling?

   b. What can we learn about the nature of vocation-calling from the vocation story of St. John Baptist de La Salle?

5) What is most helpful from the various stories for your own calling, your own journey to purpose?

6) What questions do you have about the nature of vocation-calling—i.e., the principles and processes for clarifying and pursuing a vocation-calling?

7) What additional resources do you want or need to help support your journey?

8) What next, best step can you take to help you further clarify and pursue a calling? (And then repeat....)

For Further Exploration

Adams, Kathleen. *Journal to the Self: Twenty-two Paths to Personal Growth.* Grand Central, 1990.

Cahalan, Kathleen A., and Bonnie J. Miller-McLemore, eds. *Calling All Years Good: Christian Vocation throughout Life's Seasons.* McLemore, Wm. B. Eerdmans Publishing, 2017.

Cahalan, Kathleen A., and Douglas J. Schurrman, eds. *Calling in Today's World: Voices from Eight Faith Perspectives.* Wm.B. Eerdmans Publishing, 2016.

Callings: NetVUE Podcast Series. Conversations on college, career, and a life well-lived. "Callings" explores what it means to live a life defined by a sense of meaning and purpose. It focuses on the process of exploring and discerning one's vocation, with particular emphasis on mentoring and supporting undergraduate students as they navigate college, career, and a life-well lived. Hosted by the Network for Vocation in Undergraduate Education (NetVUE). https://vocationmatters. org/2020/10/21/callings-netvues-podcast-series/

Doty, James R. *Into the Magic Shop: A Neurosurgeon's Quest to Discover the Mysteries of the Brain and Secrets of the Heart.* Avery, 2017.

Kennedy, Sheila M., and Br. Philip Johnson, FSC, eds. *Journeys to Purpose: The DISCOVER Stories Project* [Volume 1], Lewis University, 2019.

Kirabo, Noeline. "Two Questions to Uncover Your Passion—and Turn It into a Career." *TEDWomen*, 2019. https://www.ted.com/talks/noeline_kirabo_2_questions_to_uncover_your_passion_and_turn_it_into_a_career

Lewis University's Career Services and DISCOVER Online Resources: Career Services site: https://www.lewisu.edu/resources/careerservices/index.htm
DISCOVER Resources Guide: https://lewisu.libguides.com/c.php?g=426015
DISCOVER Vocation Resources Library: https://lewisu.libguides.com/discover
DISCOVER webpage: https://www.lewisu.edu/discover/

The Marginalian, by Maria Popova: https://www.themarginalian.org/
An engaging, interdisciplinary chronicle of the author's reckoning of "what it means to live a tender, thoughtful life of purpose and gladness... intellectually, creatively, spiritually, poetically... on the search for meaning across science, art, philosophy, and the various other tendrils of human thought and feeling...."

McAdams, Dan, and Jennifer Guo. "How Shall I Live? Constructing a Life Story in the College Years." *New Directions in Higher Education*, Volume 2014, Issue 166, Special Issue: *In Search of Self: Exploring Student Identity Development*, Summer 2014, pp 15-23. https://doi.org/10.1002/he.20091

Muldoon, Tim. *Living Against the Grain: How to Make Decisions that Lead to an Authentic Life.* Loyola Press, 2017.

On Being with Krista Tippet Podcast Series. "On Being is a conversation that has been building for over two decades with wise and graceful lives—across spiritual inquiry and science, social healing and the arts [including the] Peabody award-winning show that began on public radio—now podcasting a season of new shows every spring and fall." https://onbeing.org/series/podcast/

Palmer, Parker. *Let Your Life Speak: Listening for the Voice of Vocation.* Jossey-Bass, 2000.

Reyes, Patrick B. *The Purpose Gap: Empowering Communities of Color to Find Meaning and Thrive.* West Minster John Knox Press, 2021.

Salm, Luke. *The Work is Yours.* Christian Brothers Conference, 1996.

The School of Life. A global organization based in London, "The School of Life is an organization built to help us find calm, self-understanding, resilience, and connection...." Resources focus on six themes: Self-Knowledge, Relationships, Work, Calm, Leisure, Sociability, including the following publications: *Self-Knowledge, Who Am I?, A Job to Love,* and *The Career Workbook.* www.theschooloflife.com

Schwen, Mark R., and Dorothy C. Bass, eds. *Leading Lives that Matter: What We Should Do and How We Should Be.* 2nd edition, Wm. B. Eerdmans, 2020.

Smith, Emily Esfahani. "There's More to Life than Being Happy." *TEDTalk,* 2017. https://www.ted.com/talks/emily_esfahani_smith_there_s_more_to_life_than_being_happy?language=en

—-. "The Two Kinds of Stories We Tell about Ourselves." *Ideas.TED.Com.* Jan. 12, 2017. https://ideas.ted.com/the-two-kinds-of-stories-we-tell-about-ourselves/

Vocation Matters [blog]: Insights and Conversation from the Network for Vocation in Undergraduate Education (NetVUE). https://vocationmatters.org/

Wapnick, Emilie. "Why Some of Us Don't Have One True Calling." *TEDx,* 2015. https://www.ted.com/talks/emilie_wapnick_why_some_of_us_don_t_have_one_true_calling

About DISCOVER

DISCOVER is a university-wide initiative designed to help undergraduate students explore and discern a vocation or calling for their lives—that is, to live and work with meaning and generous purpose.

Created in 2010, and with ongoing, generous support from the Lilly Endowment and the Council of Independent College's Network for Vocation in Undergraduate Education, DISCOVER seeks to cultivate a campus-wide culture of vocation and calling, supporting students as they discover who they are and how they might use their unique gifts to help create a better world.

DISCOVER's primary areas of focus include:

- Curricular opportunities and enhancements through one-credit workshops and vocation-centered content integrated into existing courses and supported by faculty mini-grants.

- Student retreat opportunities, including vocation-themed retreats.

- Faculty and staff reflection opportunities, including an annual end-of-year retreat co-sponsored with the Office of Mission and Identity; and writing vocation life stories for the publication *Journeys to Purpose: The DISCOVER Stories Project.* In turn, the publication is a featured text in the Cornerstone Seminar for first-year and transfer students.

- Vocation-centered academic advising and career counseling.

- The development of vocation-centered library and online resources available to all.

DISCOVER advances and promotes the University's understanding of vocation and calling as it relates to our Catholic Lasallian Mission and is inspired by:

- The story of Saint John Baptist de La Salle, the Patron Saint of Educators and founder of the De La Salle Christian Brothers.

- The intersection of the liberal arts curriculum and professional preparation as identified in the Lewis University Mission Statement.

- The gifts of the University's Catholic and Lasallian values.

- The opportunity that the college experience provides to students searching for meaning and purpose in their lives.